Bible Fun Stuff

FOR AGES 5-7

Crafty Cookin'

David C Cook®

transforming lives together

CRAFTY COOKIN'
Published by David C. Cook
4050 Lee Vance View
Colorado Springs, CO 80918 U.S.A.

David C. Cook Distribution Canada
55 Woodslee Avenue, Paris, Ontario, Canada N3L 3E5

David C. Cook U.K., Kingsway Communications
Eastbourne, East Sussex BN23 6NT, England

Written by Heather Tietz
Cover Design by BMB Design/Scott Johnson
Interior Design by TrueBlue Design/Sandy Flewelling
Photography © Brad Armstrong Photography
Illustrations by Aline Heiser, Mark Stay, Marguerite Voisey,
Only Vectors | Dreamstime.com

ISBN 978-1-4347-6719-6

Printed in the United States
First Printing 2009

1 2 3 4 5 6 7 8 9 10

transforming lives together

Table of Contents

Scrumptious Sunday School

Jelly. Pretzels. Bananas. Open your kitchen cupboards. Get ready to mix, squash, crush, roll, and pour some of the most commonplace foods into fun! Turn your classroom into a tantalizing place. With these 26 simple cooking adventures, your 5- to 7-year-old students will get to taste and see that God is truly good.

Each lesson is a genuine hands-on learning experience. From their noses to their toes, all of the students' five senses will be involved. Your young chefs will be motivated to listen and learn. They'll be crafting scrumptious desserts and transforming healthy ingredients into irresistible fun. Some snacks will be for sharing. Others will be group projects. The sights, sounds, scents, taste, and feel of each activity will make mouthwatering memories. Your Bible lessons will be unforgettable and delicious!

Making Your Lessons Stick To Kids' Hearts
(and not to your floor)

The 26 activities in this book can be done in any order and easily fit into any curriculum. Simply use the Scripture and Topic Index on page 110 to match a project with the lesson you're teaching. These activities also can be used as alternate Step Three activities in several curriculum lines: David C. Cook Bible-in-Life, Echoes, LifeLINKS to God, College Press, Reformation Press, Wesley, Anglican, and The Cross. If you have one of these lines, look through the Correlation Chart on page 111 and find the activity geared to your lesson. You'll use this new activity instead of one of the other Step Three activities listed in your teacher's guide. This book, when combined with *Fizz, Foam, & Froth Science Lab*, will give you a full year's worth of Step Three replacement activities for the early elementary age group.

Here are a few general tips as you proceed:

Disinfecting wipes are a necessity. Be sure that students' hands are clean prior to beginning every activity. Hand wipes to students as they enter the room or place them at their seats. If your classroom lacks a sink, a small basin of water and a hand towel will be helpful. After the activity, students might need to wash off ingredients before cleaning their hands again with a wipe.

Aprons are also practical; nothing ruins the effect of a great lesson like a spill. Ask parents to send in used adult-size shirts to protect their children's clothes. T-shirts can be cut down the back, then pinned shut with a clothespin.

Prior to the start of each lesson, present the Scripture to your students. Use a picture book, flannel board, props, or other visual aid to help your students see the story. It is also helpful to use a signal to call to order. Grab a bell, a kazoo, or other sound maker to get children's attention. A silent hand raise or a special clap pattern can also let them know when to STOP and LISTEN.

Prepare yourself by reading each lesson's Bible Snack; this will give you a dab of history behind each Scripture. When you gather supplies for each lesson, plan a little extra to use for demonstration.

Most importantly, take note of students' allergies. The lessons have alternative ingredients for the most common allergies—milk, wheat, and peanuts. If you are ever in doubt about the safety of an ingredient, check with the parent. We have included an allergy alert letter on page 112.

So, open your cupboards and turn the page. You and your students are in for some delicious fun!

Cookie Faces

Design a GRRRReat cookie animal face.

Bible Basis: Genesis 1:20-25

MEMORY VERSE: Everything God created is good. 1 Timothy 4:4

 ## Bible Snack

God is orderly. The world He put together is like an intricate machine, each piece relying on others to make it work properly. The order of creation testifies to God's care for organization. Light, water, and land—those things necessary for growth—came prior to plant life. Animals followed. The vegetation made food and shelter available for them once they entered the scene. These ecosystems balanced plant and animal life so the giving and taking from the earth would be orderly. Day and night established regular rest cycles for the animals and also allowed for greater diversity among species. Then God created human beings last, knowing that they would need all these things to sustain their lives.

With His incredible power and imagination, God made an amazing variety of creatures. Think of the differences in just some of God's creation: God created ants to lift many times their own weight with their mouths and adult giraffes to have tongues an average of 27 inches long! Our wonderful God is truly creative! Help your students learn to worship almighty God for His awesome creative power.

CRAFTER SUPPLIES

- ☐ 1 plain 2" sugar cookie
- ☐ 1 donut hole or small cookie
- ☐ Paper cup with: 2 round-hole candies, 3 chocolate chips, and a 1" strand of red licorice
- ☐ Paper plate

GROUP SUPPLIES

- ☐ Plastic knives or craft sticks (1 per 2 chefs)
- ☐ White icing (about 3 tbsp. per chef)
- ☐ Shredded orange coconut (2 tbsp. per chef)

TEACHER SUPPLIES

- ☐ Yellow and red food coloring

Mess Management

- If desired, instead of store-bought cookies, you can make 2" diameter sugar cookies. Refrigerating the dough for 20 minutes before baking helps cookies retain their shape.

- One donut hole can be substituted for the small cookie. If using these, cut each in half. Then divide one of the halves again.

- Use licorice that peels apart. Separate strands ahead of time. You'll need a strand for each chef.

- Add one drop each of yellow and red food coloring to the shredded coconut. Mix well to create an orange color.

- Fill one 5 oz. paper cup per child as directed in CRAFTER SUPPLIES.

- Use a dab of icing to hold any items that won't easily stay in place.

ALLERGY WARNING: *If you have a chef who is allergic to peanuts, handling the candy or coconut could be dangerous. Allow him to decorate his cookie with fruit pieces, such as grape halves and blueberries, or dried fruit.*

 ## Appetizer

God made big, small, furry, slimy, quiet, and loud animals. What other types of animals are there? (animals that prefer the cold, others that like heat, etc.) Do you have a favorite animal?

 ## Instructions

Grow Bear's Hair:

❶ Use the knife or craft stick to spread icing on the top of your cookie. Be sure to spread the icing onto the edges too.

❷ Roll your cookie like a wheel in the coconut. This is your bear's fur.

Create the Face:

❶ Put a small bit of icing on the back of a small cookie (or the sliced edge of a donut hole half). Place it in the center of the cookie.

❷ Find a chocolate chip. Push the pointed side down into the little cookie (or donut hole). This is the bear's nose.

❸ Find the two round candies. Press these above the nose. These are the bear's eyes.

❹ Find two more chocolate chips. Put a little bit of icing on the pointed ends. Place them in the holes of the round candies.

❺ Add the licorice piece for a mouth.

Add the Ears:

❶ Take your other little cookie (or donut pieces) and cut it in half. Set the pieces on your plate, above the eyes. These are the bear's ears.

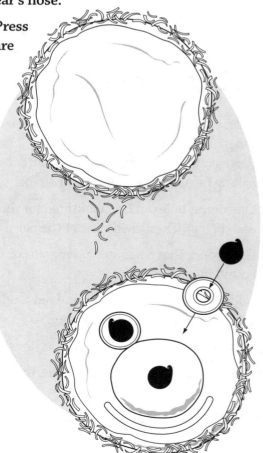

 **Dessert**

❶ **What different types of animals did God create?** (Answers should cover livestock, creatures that move along the ground, and wild animals.)

❷ **What is your favorite animal that God created?** (Encourage each child to briefly share something.)

Dear God, You are creative! We are so glad the world is filled with different kinds of animals. This world You made is a wonderful, fascinating place to be! In Jesus' name we pray, amen.

Popcorn Ball World

Squeeze together a tasty world.

Bible Basis: Genesis 1:26–31; 2:7–8, 15, 18–23

MEMORY VERSE: Everything God created is good. 1 Timothy 4:4

 ## Bible Snack

The name Eden comes from the Hebrew word for *delight*. It isn't clear exactly where the Garden of Eden was located. However, Scripture does say that a river flowed out of it and that two of its branches were called the Tigris and Euphrates. It is possible that this lush garden covered the land anywhere from Africa to Iraq.

When God finished the last day of creation, He looked at all He had made and it was very good. This most significant day was when He created humankind. God made man and woman in His image. By taking woman out of man and not out of the earth, God unified the two. He gave them authority over all the earth, to care for it.

This assignment was given prior to the first sin. This work was not a punishment. Rather, it was an honor to be entrusted with the intricate life that God had so lovingly made. Nature serves us daily by producing our food and housing, cleansing our air, recycling our water, and by providing serenity and entertainment. God's love for us is shown even through this. Caring for our world is an act of love toward Him.

CRAFTER SUPPLIES

- ☐ Paper bowl
- ☐ 5 oz. paper cup filled with: 1 tsp. of chocolate chips, 1 tsp. of round, blue candy

GROUP SUPPLIES

- ☐ Bowl of whole wheat cereal (about 2 heaping tbsp. per chef)
- ☐ Bowl of rice flakes cereal (about 2 heaping tbsp. per chef)
- ☐ Bowl of popcorn (about 1 heaping tbsp. per chef)
- ☐ Colored sprinkles (about 1 tsp. per chef)
- ☐ Several tablespoons for each snack bowl

TEACHER SUPPLIES

- ☐ Cooking spray
- ☐ Marshmallow cream
- ☐ Metal spoon

Mess Management

- Prepare one 5 oz. paper cup per chef as directed in CRAFTER SUPPLIES.

- Spoon two tablespoons of marshmallow cream into each chef's bowl just prior to the activity.

ALLERGY WARNING: *If you have chefs who are allergic to wheat or peanuts, this craft could be dangerous for them. Have them use the popcorn and rice cereal with the marshmallow cream to make the worlds. They can use colored sugar sprinkles instead of candy sprinkles, chocolate chips, or blue candies.*

 # Appetizer

After God made the world, He called it very good. Have you ever made something you thought was very good? (a drawing or painting, a craft, a song, etc.) Did you take good care of what you made?

 # Instructions

Squeeze a World:

❶ Put two spoonfuls of the cereal and then popcorn into your bowl with the marshmallow cream. When you are done, open your hands flat so your palms face the ceiling. Demonstrate this. Spray each chef's palms and fingers with cooking spray once children are finished with the task.

❷ Next, you are going to make a little world. Use both hands and squeeze your ingredients into a tight ball.

❸ When you have a tight ball, set your world in your bowl.

Add Life:

❶ Take turns spooning sprinkles onto your world. These can be miniature plants, animals, and people.

Create Features:

❶ Find your chocolate chips; these are miniature mountains. Stick them onto your world.

❷ Find your blue candies; these are lakes and seas. Stick them onto your world too.

 ## Dessert

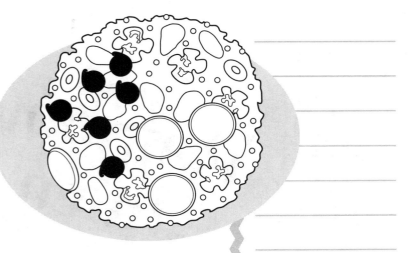

- **When God made the world, He gave two people the job of caring for it. Who were they?** (Adam and Eve.)

- **Who should care for the world today?** (You and me.) **How can we do that?** (treat animals kindly, don't litter, water plants, recycle, etc.)

Dear God, what a beautiful world You've made! You want us to care for it. We need to treat Your animals and plants, Your land and water with care. Help us understand how to do that. In Jesus' name we pray, amen.

Rainbow Juice

Everyone helps concoct this rainbow of fruit.

Bible Basis:
Genesis 6:5–
22; 7:11–17, 24

MEMORY VERSE:
*We know and rely on
the love God has for
us. 1 John 4:16*

 ## Bible Snack

God's eyes are always searching for the righteous. Throughout the Bible are stories of God's preservation of a righteous remnant. The first account of this is in Genesis; Noah was a righteous man who walked with God.

The ark that God asked Noah to build was as long as about one and a half football fields and taller than a four-story building. It has been calculated that the ark would have had room for about 7,000 species. Noah faithfully constructed the ark for 120 years before it began to rain. Water from the heavens as well as water from the oceans, rivers, seas, and deep springs (Gen. 7:11) combined to cover the earth. Though it rained for only 40 days, Noah and his family spent about a year after that simply waiting for the floodwaters to recede (Gen. 8:14–19).

Accounts of catastrophic floods are preserved in both written and oral traditions throughout the world. Many recount the building of a giant boat and the preservation of only a few people. The New Testament, as well, refers back to the story of the flood (Matt. 24:38; Luke 17:26–27; Heb. 11:7; 1 Pet. 3:20; and 2 Pet. 2:5). Jesus, like the great ark, is a sure salvation for those who enter in.

CRAFTER SUPPLIES

- [ ] 5 oz. paper cup filled with: a halved straw and 1" colored fruit pieces such as large grapes, banana slices, and strawberries

GROUP SUPPLIES

- [ ] Banana
- [ ] ¼ c. diced pear
- [ ] ¼ c. green seedless grapes
- [ ] ½ c. blueberries
- [ ] 1 c. strawberries
- [ ] 1 ½ c. apple juice

TEACHER SUPPLIES

- [ ] Blender

Mess Management

- Bring a blender to class.
- This recipe makes about 3 ½ cups of juice or 28 ounces.
- Wash the fruit well to rinse off any pesticides and dirt. Adding a tablespoon of vinegar to the wash water would be an extra step of caution. Rinse well.
- Cut one straw in half for each chef, half for skewering and half for drinking.
- Cut fruit into 1" pieces. Each chef will need three different colored fruits to string onto his or her straw.
- Prepare one 5 oz. paper cup per chef as specified in CRAFTER SUPPLIES.
- Because the fruit in this drink will stain carpets, if possible have your chefs carry their cups onto a hard floor or outside to pour and enjoy. As always, donning aprons is a wise precaution.

ALLERGY WARNING: *Be sure students with any fruit allergies avoid touching or using fruits they are sensitive to. If a student must avoid corn syrup, be sure you use 100% juice and read the label before using.*

 # Appetizer

Noah and his family were on the ark for more than a year. When they got off the boat, God gave them a beautiful gift—a rainbow. Have you seen a rainbow? What was it like? (faint, colorful, beautiful, in the shape of an arch, etc.)

 # Instructions

String a Rainbow:

❶ **Look into your paper cup. Take out your straw. Push each piece of your fruit onto your straw. You will make a rainbow.**

❷ **God gave a rainbow to Noah and his family. What did it remind them of?** (God would never flood the world again.)

Blend a Rainbow:

❶ **When you are finished, raise your hand.** Call on quiet students to come up and add some fruit to the blender in this order: 1 cup strawberries, a banana, ¼ cup diced pear, ¼ cup green seedless grapes, and ½ cup blueberries.

❷ **Can everyone see the rainbow we've made? Rainbows can remind us that God cares about our safety.** Pour enough apple juice into the blender to cover the fruit, about 1½ cups. Blend until smooth.

Drink a Rainbow:

❶ **Hold your paper cup with both hands. I'm going to come around and pour you a rainbow.** Pour and enjoy the drink using the rainbow straws.

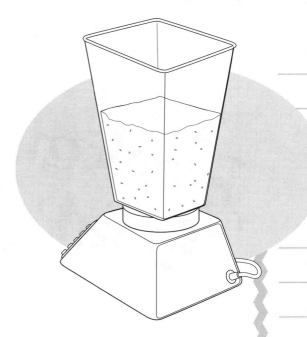

 # Dessert

- **Why did God tell Noah to build an ark?** (God was going to flood the earth with water. God cared about Noah's safety.)

- **How did God keep Noah safe?** (By telling Noah what to do to be safe.)

Dear God, You are so big! You can see what everyone is doing all the time. Just as with Noah and his family, You can tell us how to be safe. Help us listen to Your quiet voice and obey You. Thank You for caring about our safety. In Jesus' name we pray, amen.

Basket Boat

Baby Moses is kept safe in this fun boat!

Bible Basis: Exodus 1:6–2:10

MEMORY VERSE: Let us love one another, for love comes from God. 1 John 4:7

 ## Bible Snack

Moses was born during a time of political unrest. More than 600,000 Israelites were living in Egypt under Pharaoh (Num. 1:45–46). The peace and privilege gained from Joseph's management of Egypt years before (Gen. 47:5) had been forgotten. Now the Israelites were seen as a threat. The new pharaoh feared they might join with enemies from the north and overtake Egypt, so he enslaved them. It is probable that the Israelites built the great pyramids. They were also carpenters, jewelers, and craftsmen for the Egyptians.

Though oppressed, the Israelites continued to grow in number. The fearful pharaoh ordered the Hebrew midwives to kill all Hebrew newborn baby boys. When the midwives defied Pharaoh and let the newborns live, Pharaoh put this death request into the hands of his people. This is where Moses' story begins.

When Moses was three months old, his mother fashioned a boat-like basket from papyrus reeds, waterproofed it, and set it along the Nile. This was the very place where babies were being discarded. Possibly Moses' mother knew where the pharaoh's daughter came to bathe. She strategically left Moses there with her daughter, Miriam, to stand guard. All but Moses' voice would have been camouflaged among the tall papyrus reeds.

Fear motivated Pharaoh to oppress the Israelites. Love motivated Moses' family to do all they could to save him. Love can be as strategic as hateful fear. God blessed Moses' family's effort to care for him.

CRAFTER SUPPLIES

- ☐ Paper plate
- ☐ 1 waffle bowl
- ☐ ½ of a banana
- ☐ 6" strip of fruit leather
- ☐ Craft stick or plastic knife

GROUP SUPPLIES

- ☐ Pretzel sticks
- ☐ Mini chocolate chips
- ☐ Bowls

TEACHER SUPPLIES

- ☐ Marshmallow cream
- ☐ Scissors
- ☐ Tablespoon

Mess Management

- Purchase the fruit leather in strips so that it is quicker to cut. Cut one 6" strip of fruit leather per chef. Kitchen scissors are the quickest way to do this. Be sure to leave the plastic backing on.

- Separate pretzels and chocolate chips into two bowls.

- Place a waffle bowl open side up on each plate and put about 2 tbsp. marshmallow cream inside each cone.

- Keep the marshmallow cream at room temperature so it is easier to spread.

ALLERGY WARNING: *If you have a chef who is allergic to peanuts, handling chocolate chips could be dangerous for him. Instead he could use raisins or pieces of fresh fruit, such as blueberries, grape halves, or strawberry pieces.*

 # Appetizer

Moses had a wonderful big sister, Miriam. When he was just a tiny baby, she helped her mother save his life! How does your family keep you safe? (has rules, stays close by when I'm playing, takes me to the doctor, etc.)

 # Instructions

Put Moses in the Boat:

❶ Baby Moses was very loved. His mother made a soft place in the basket for him to lie. **I will come around and give you a nice soft place for your baby Moses.** Spoon 2 tbsp. of marshmallow cream into each waffle bowl basket boat.

❷ His mother then carefully put baby Moses in the boat. **Peel your banana and put it in the boat to be baby Moses. You can add mini chocolate chips for eyes if you'd like.**

❸ Find your fruit strip. Peel off the plastic. **Lay your fruit strip over baby Moses in the basket like a blanket. Or if you like, you may wrap the blanket around him instead.** Demonstrate this.

Add the Reeds:

❶ **Who watched over Moses in his little basket?** (His sister Miriam.) **His basket floated in the Nile River, hidden among the**

reeds along the river's edge.
Take a few pretzels sticks and place
them upright along the edge of your
bowl. Demonstrate this. **These are
the reeds in the river.**

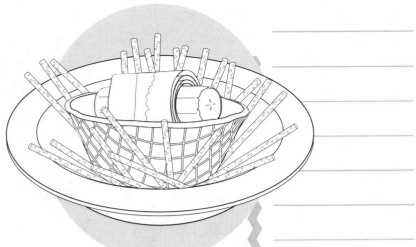

❷ Your basket boat can be a reminder
that God gave you a family to care
for you too!

 # Dessert

● **How did Moses' mother care for Moses?** (She hid him in a basket on a river
to keep him safe from Pharaoh.)

● **God wants people in families to care for one another. What are some
ways you can show each person in your family that you care about him or
her?** (spend time with him or her, obey my parents, share toys with my
siblings, help with chores, help a younger sibling get dressed, etc.)

Dear God, You are King of all! If I am Your child, You will take care of me.
Thank You for my family. Help me show my family I love them today. In
Jesus' name we pray, amen.

Family Circles

Create a family portrait with these little veggie sandwiches.

Bible Basis:
Exodus 18

MEMORY VERSE:
Let us love one another, for love comes from God.
1 John 4:7

 ## Bible Snack

Like a gourmet chef at work, God purposefully plans families. He knows what steaming concoctions are created when different personalities mix. He knows the hard-to-swallow lessons of patience, forgiveness, humility, and self-denial that come from family interactions. He designed families to give us a taste of His love.

Moses had two families as a child. He grew up as an adopted son of an Egyptian princess. He had an Egyptian education (Acts 7:22) and was catered to as a prince. But, he was also a Hebrew, cared for in his infancy by his Hebrew mother (Exod. 2:1–10). When Moses fled 200 miles to Midian after killing an Egyptian, he became part of another family. This semi-nomadic people taught him the wilderness lifestyle. He learned to shepherd, an occupation that had been despised in Egypt (Gen. 46:34). He also learned more about the God of his ancestors, whom his father-in-law, Jethro, worshiped. Forty years later, Moses would welcome Jethro's advice about judging the disagreements of the Hebrew people.

God used the influence of each family to develop Moses into the strong, knowledgeable, godly leader who led the Hebrew people out of Egypt and through the wilderness.

CRAFTER SUPPLIES

- ☐ 1 tortilla
- ☐ Plastic knife or craft stick
- ☐ Paper plate

GROUP SUPPLIES

- ☐ Different size circular cookie cutters from about 1 ½ to 3" (about 1 per 2 chefs)
- ☐ Softened cream cheese
- ☐ Various toppings: shredded carrot, shredded cheese, sliced olives, thin sliced sandwich meat, halved grape tomatoes, cucumbers

TEACHER SUPPLIES

- ☐ Cheese grater
- ☐ Knife
- ☐ Cutting board

Mess Management

- Shred the carrot and cheese.
- Slice the olives.
- Slice the tomatoes in half and cut the cucumbers into very thin 1" slices for mouths.
- If you don't have circle cookie cutters, plastic and glass cups can also be used to cut circles out of the tortilla.

ALLERGY WARNING: *If you have any chefs that are lactose intolerant, use nondairy options (marshmallow cream, mayonnaise, margarine) for the cream cheese. Chefs with wheat allergies could decorate small rice cakes or circular slices of apple or cucumber instead.*

 # Appetizer

Jethro taught Moses how to help the Israelites with their problems. What has your family taught you to do? (how to ride a bike, how to read, how to speak another language, how to share, etc.)

 # Instructions

Cut Circle Faces:

❶ Find your tortilla. Choose one cookie cutter. Place it along the edge of one tortilla. Cut out a circle. Be sure to press down hard and turn the cutter back and forth. Demonstrate this.

❷ Choose another cookie cutter and make two more circles.

❸ Set aside the leftover tortilla. Place your circles on your plate. These are your faces.

Design Your Family:

❶ Spread the cream cheese onto each tortilla circle.

❷ Choose a vegetable or cheese for hair.

❸ Use more vegetable pieces to make eyes and a mouth on each face.

 **Dessert**

- **How did Moses learn from Jethro?** (Moses learned by having Jethro watch him work and then listening to Jethro's advice.)
- **What things have you learned from your family?** (Allow each chef to share one thing learned.)

Dear God, thank You for my family. You put us together. We have a lot to learn from each other. Help me remember that each person in my family can help make me a better person. In Jesus' name we pray, amen.

Crunchy Cracker Commandments

Write with jelly and remember God's commands!

Bible Basis:
Exodus 19:1-25; 20:1-17

MEMORY VERSE:
The LORD will indeed give what is good.
Psalm 85:12

 ## Bible Snack

The Ten Commandments can be summed up in one word—LOVE. The first four commandments deal with how to love God. The remaining six commandments show us how to love others. Over time Jewish leaders reconstructed the commandments into a list of regulations. Jesus reprimanded the Pharisees who were so prudent about following the law and enforcing it on others. Jesus said that He hadn't come to do away with the Law of Moses, but to fulfill it (Matt. 5:17). That's just what Jesus did; His main mission was to love His Father and to love people.

God gave His commandments to the Israelites. He wanted them to be a special kingdom, a group of people who could approach God and demonstrate His love and forgiveness to the world. God's plan was that "all nations on earth" (Gen. 18:18) would be blessed through them. The Israelites were to be a light to the world, showing others how to live right and love God. The Israelites were also to be the people to produce the Messiah. Jews and Gentiles, kings and commoners—everyone— could then come to know and love the God who made them.

CRAFTER SUPPLIES

- ☐ Paper plate
- ☐ 1 graham cracker, halved
- ☐ Knife
- ☐ Plastic bag with the corner clipped and 3 tbsp. jelly inside

GROUP SUPPLIES

- ☐ Bowl of 8 oz. cream cheese whipped with ¼ c. orange juice

TEACHER SUPPLIES

- ☐ Fork or mixer
- ☐ Scissors

Mess Management

- Carefully break the graham crackers in half, so each chef has two squares.

- Use a fork or a mixer to blend the cream cheese and orange juice. This will make the cream cheese easier to spread.

- Prepare one plastic zip closure bag for each chef as specified in CRAFTER SUPPLIES. Clip just a bit of the corner with scissors to create a tiny opening, about ⅛".

ALLERGY WARNING: *If you have chefs who are allergic to milk, nondairy whipped cream can be substituted for the cream cheese. For chefs who are allergic to citrus, use a bit of milk or apple juice to thin the cream cheese.*

 # Appetizer

Rules help keep us safe and happy. God gave us rules. Can you name any of God's rules? (don't steal, don't lie, don't kill, love, etc.) **What rule do you think is most important?** (Love God.)

 # Instructions

Make the Tablets:

❶ Use your plastic knife. Carefully spread the cream cheese mixture on your two graham crackers. These are like the two stone tablets God gave Moses. **What was on these tablets?** (The Ten Commandments, God's rules.)

Write with Jelly:

❶ **How many commands did God gives Moses?** (10) We can remember one word to help us keep all ten commands. That word is LOVE. You can either write the letters L-O-V-E or you can draw a heart.

❷ Find your jelly bag. This is what you can write with. Look for the cut corner of your bag. Gently squeeze the jelly into that corner. Demonstrate how to hold the bag.

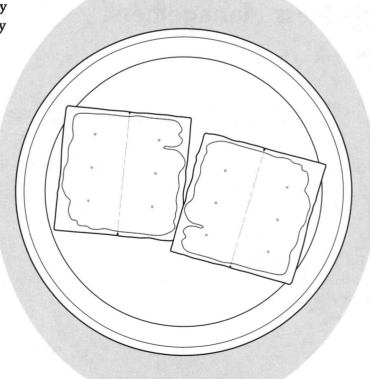

❸ Next, carefully squeeze the jelly out onto your graham cracker tablets. If some students are unable to "write" with the jelly, allow them to use their finger like a paintbrush instead.

 ## Dessert

● **Why did God give us rules?** (So we know how to please God, be happy, and get along with others.)

● **What are some of the rules God gave us?** (Let chefs share any of the commandments.)

Dear God, You love us so much! Thank You for giving us Your commandments. They help us know how to love. Help us love the people we are with today. In Jesus' name we pray, amen.

Wise Apple Owl

Whoo, whoo likes caramel and apples?

**Bible Basis:
1 Kings 3:1-15**

*MEMORY VERSE:
Love the Lord your
God with all your
heart.*
Matthew 22:37

 ## Bible Snack

Solomon began his reign with a selfless request. He was in his early twenties. His father, David, had led the Israelites as a righteous king who'd made the worship of God of foremost importance. Solomon had been entrusted with a huge responsibility. His prayer was humble. He acknowledged that God had given him the job of ruling over His people.

Solomon was eager for the wisdom to rule righteously. He wanted the knowledge and understanding that would enable him to make correct judgments and excellent decisions. God granted his request abundantly. His wise decisions led to treaties that helped him keep peace with the surrounding nations. His reputation for wisdom drew leaders from afar to visit him.

Unfortunately Solomon did not maintain a life of making good choices. He allowed pagan worship to creep into his kingdom through his many marriages to foreign women. This lessened his devotion to God. His writing of the Book of Ecclesiastes later in his life reflects the emptiness that even the wealthiest, wisest man can experience when God is no longer a priority.

CRAFTER SUPPLIES

☐ Apple half

☐ 5 oz. paper cup filled
   with: 1 orange slice
   halved into 2 triangles,
   2 toothpicks, 2 dried
   apricots, 2 raisins, and
   2 candy corns

GROUP SUPPLIES

☐ Bowl of caramel (about
   ¼ c. per 3 chefs)

TEACHER SUPPLIES

☐ Knife

☐ Cutting board

☐ Plastic storage container

☐ Lemon juice

Mess Management

- Cut an apple half for each chef. Remove the core and seeds. Slice the bottom and top off so that each end is flat. If they will be stored overnight, add 2 tablespoons lemon juice to the storage container.

- Prepare one 5 oz. paper cup per chef as specified in CRAFTER SUPPLIES.

- Prepare a bowl of caramel for dipping as specified in GROUP SUPPLIES.

- If the caramel isn't sticking the apricots or other items to the apple, simply use more toothpicks to hold them in place.

ALLERGY WARNING: *If you have a chef who is allergic to peanuts, handling the raisins, other dried fruit, or candy might be dangerous for him. Instead, he could make eyes with globs of cream cheese. Jelly can be added to create the pupils. Carrot pieces could make a beak.*

 # Appetizer

I am going to describe a creature to you. Can you guess it? It's a kind of bird. In some stories this bird is so wise that other animals ask him for help with their problems. What animal is this? (Owl.)

One man in the Bible asked God to make him wise. He was so wise people came to him for help with their problems. Who was he? (Solomon.)

 # Instructions

Make the Wings:

❶ Look at your orange slices. What shape are they? (Triangles.) **Find the peel. Stick a toothpick through the thin end of the peel.** Demonstrate this.

❷ **Keep pushing the toothpick so it pokes into the top side of the apple. These make the wings.** Demonstrate this step.

Make the Eyes:

❶ **Dip one flat side of your apricots in the caramel. These are the owl's eyes.**

❷ **Place each apricot eye on the top of the apple.**

❸ **Dip each raisin in the caramel. Place one in the middle of each of the apricot eyes.**

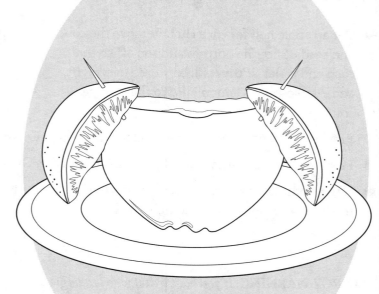

Make the Beak:

❶ Find two candy corns. Stick the pointed ends in the center of the apple peel. One candy corn will go above the other. These make the owl's beak. Demonstrate this step. You may have to help students with this step by using a toothpick to make a hole for the candy corns to stick into.

 Dessert

God gave Solomon a wise and understanding heart. He used that wisdom to make good choices.

● **Why did God give Solomon more than wisdom?** (God was pleased that Solomon made a good choice by asking for wisdom.)

● **What do you think are some good choices you can make?** (Answers will vary.)

Dear God, making good choices can be so hard. Thank You that we can always ask You for help to make a good choice. Help us remember to talk to You when we have big choices to make. In Jesus' name we pray, amen.

Bread Bed Roll

Roll up a tasty tortilla sandwich.

Bible Basis:
2 Kings 4:8–13

MEMORY VERSE:
The LORD will indeed give what is good.
Psalm 85:12

Bible Snack

God cares about where we live. Scripture is filled with accounts of God's provision of food and shelter for His people. While the Israelites wandered through the wilderness, God fed them with the nourishing, honey-like manna for 40 years. Ravens, sent by God, delivered food to the prophet Elijah. Later Elijah received meals from a poor widow to whom God had given an unending jar of flour and oil (1 Kings 17:4, 15–16).

Elisha was Elijah's successor. Though he came from a wealthy family, Elisha trusted in God to provide for him as he traveled extensively. God directed a Shunammite woman to make a bed-and-breakfast suite on her roof for Elisha so he would have accommodations whenever he passed through her town of Shunem. In Bible times, the roof of a home was commonly used to pray, relax, or even pitch a tent. In return for her kindness, God gave the woman a son, as prophesied by Elisha (2 Kings 4:16–17). God blessed this woman and her home because she graciously shared it through hospitality to a godly man.

CRAFTER SUPPLIES

- [ ] Small tortilla, cut into a rectangle shape
- [ ] ½ cheese stick
- [ ] Craft stick or plastic knife
- [ ] Toothpick

GROUP SUPPLIES

- [ ] Rectangular shaped lettuce leaves
- [ ] Rectangular shaped lunch meat
- [ ] Salad dressing
- [ ] Margarine

TEACHER SUPPLIES

- [ ] Knife
- [ ] Cutting board

Mess Management

- Wash and pat dry the lettuce. Cut it into rectangular shapes. Each shape should be about half the length of the tortilla. Alternately, smaller pieces of lettuce may be spread evenly over the tortilla.

- If you purchase lunch meat from a deli, be sure it is no more than three days old. It is always a good precaution to heat the meat until it is steaming hot. Then cut the lunch meat into rectangular shapes, about half the length of each tortilla. Keep it chilled until you are ready to use it.

ALLERGY WARNING: *If you have any chefs who are allergic to milk, soy cheese can be substituted for the cheese stick, or they can roll up a piece of lunch meat and use that for the pillow.*

 # Appetizer

People live in different types of houses all over the world. God gave Elisha a special place to sleep on someone's roof! Have you ever slept someplace other than a bed? (a tent, a camper, the ground, etc.)

 # Instructions

Make Your Bed:

❶ God always gave Elisha a place to sleep and eat. Today we are going to make a Bread Bed Roll to remind us that God cares where we live too.

❷ Choose either margarine or salad dressing. Use your plastic knife (or craft stick) to spread this on your tortilla rectangle. This is your bed.

❸ Place your cheese stick pillow at one end of your tortilla bed.

❹ Choose either a piece of lettuce or lunch meat for your blanket. Lay this blanket down below your cheese pillow.

Roll Up Your Bed:

❶ Find your cheese pillow. Beginning with this end of the tortilla, carefully roll until your bread bed is rolled up like a sleeping bag. Demonstrate.

❷ Push your toothpick through the roll to hold your bed closed. Demonstrate.

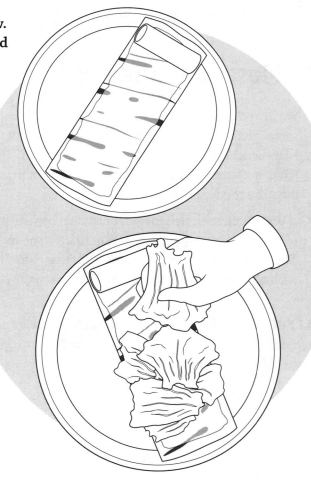

 ## Dessert

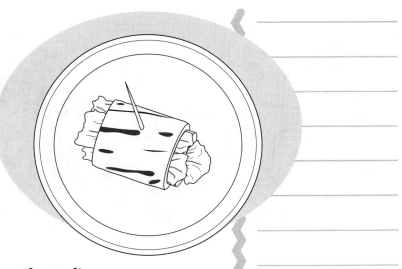

● **Why did the woman want to build a room for Elisha?** (Elisha did not have a place to stay in Shunem.)

● **How do we know that God cares about where we live?** (God cared about where Elisha lived so we know He cares about where we live too.)

Dear God, You cared that Elisha would have a place to live. Thank You for caring for me. I know that my needs are never too big or small for You. Thank You for giving me a home and caring about where I live. In Jesus' name we pray, amen.

Brownie Bible

Build a Bible with brownies and marshmallow cream.

**Bible Basis:
2 Kings 22:1-11;
23:1-3**

*MEMORY VERSE:
Love the Lord
your God with
all your heart.
Matthew 22:37*

 Bible Snack

God's law had been lost among the long line of wicked kings that ruled Judah. Amon was Josiah's father. He had turned against God and was an adamant idol worshiper. He ruled only two years before his own servants plotted his death. When his son Josiah became king, the kingdom was restored to peace. Josiah was only eight years old when he was given the throne. He began to reform the kingdom in the eighteenth year of his reign. He set about destroying the altars to Baal, the pagan shrines, Asherah poles, and other fixtures of idol worship.

Four years later Josiah took the money that the gatekeepers had collected at the temple and designated it to be used for the temple's repair. While doing this, a scroll containing the Book of the Law was found. This might have contained either the accounts of Genesis through Deuteronomy, or perhaps Deuteronomy alone. Josiah had this read to his people. They would have heard the Ten Commandments and the laws of living, which God gave to Moses. The scroll included things such as the celebration of certain annual festivals, giving of tithes, maintaining cleanliness and purity, instruction on how to rule, guidelines for worship, and the consequences for obeying and disobeying God's commands.

Josiah tore his clothes and wept at the disobedience of the former kings and of the people. His commitment to read and follow the Scriptures brought positive changes to Judah. God blessed his 30-year reign with peace and prosperity.

CRAFTER SUPPLIES

- ☐ 2 thin brownie rectangles
- ☐ Bookmark-shaped fruit leather
- ☐ Paper plate

GROUP SUPPLIES

- ☐ 1 bowl of marshmallow cream with some plastic knives

TEACHER SUPPLIES

- ☐ Knife
- ☐ Cutting board
- ☐ Brownie mix and ingredients

⚗ Mess Management

- Bake a box of brownie mix in a larger than required pan to produce thin brownies. For example, a mix meant for an 8" square pan can be baked in a 9" x 13" pan. Bake the brownies about five minutes less than required; check often to prevent burning them. A box this size will make 16 brownies, or enough for eight chefs.

- Cut one 4" fruit leather strip for each chef. Slice a small, one-centimeter triangle out of the bottom of each strip. It should resemble a bookmark.

ALLERGY WARNING: *If you have any chefs who have wheat or dairy allergies, they could decorate crispy rice treats instead. If you have a chef who is allergic to peanuts, handling the fruit leather might be dangerous for him. Instead, he could use a long slice of carrot for the bookmark.*

 # Appetizer

Josiah thought God's words were so important that he cried when he read them. The Bible is God's words. Do you have a Bible? When would be a good time for you to read from your Bible each day? (when I wake up, during breakfast, before bed, etc.)

 # Instructions

Make the Pages:

❶ Use your plastic knife to spread marshmallow cream onto each brownie. These are the pages of your Brownie Bible.

❷ Push your brownies together so they are side by side on your plate.

Add the Bookmark:

❶ Find your fruit leather bookmark. Do you see the triangle cutout? This is the bottom of the bookmark.

❷ Lay the bookmark in the middle. Slide it down. The triangle cutout should touch your plate below your brownies.

Close Your Bible:

❶ Carefully close your Brownie Bible by picking up one half and laying it down on the other half so the cream parts are together.

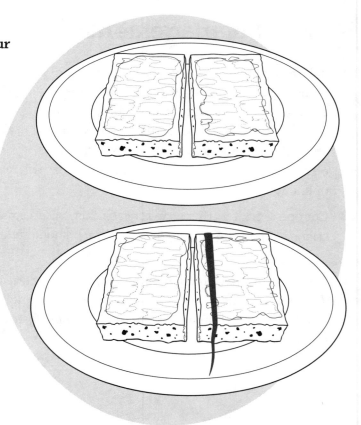

 ## Dessert

- **What did Josiah and the people do after they listened to God's Word?** (They promised to obey it.)

- **How can we listen to God's Word?** (Let volunteers share.)

Dear God, the Bible is full of Your words. Thank You for Your words to us. I want to look into the Bible often and hear Your Word. In Jesus' name we pray, amen.

Helping Hand Prints

Print your hand with the help of a friend!

Bible Basis: Mark 2:1–12

MEMORY VERSE: A friend loves at all times. Proverbs 17:17

 ## Bible Snack

The roof was a significant part of the home in Bible times. A narrow, outside stairway led from the ground to the roof. Residents used their roofs as a cool place to sit in the evening. It also was a solitary place to pray (Acts 10:9). It was the place where Hebrews built their temporary tents during the Feast of the Tabernacles (also called the Feast of Booths). Jesus even encouraged His disciples to shout His message from the housetops (Matt. 10:27).

The walls that held the roof up were constructed of stone. The roof, however, was made of chopped straw and mud. This mixture was spread over sticks and branches that were supported by wood beams.

The word *friend* is not used in this story. However, these four men showed themselves to be friends to the paralyzed man on the mat. They extended a lot of effort to bring this man to Jesus. They didn't give up when they were unable to push past the crowd. They persevered, leveraging the stretcher with the crippled man up the narrow stairway to the roof where they had to dig through the thick, sun-baked roof. Then they boldly lowered the heavy mat down into the crowded house, right at Jesus' feet. It was their faith that Jesus responded to. Jesus healed the paralyzed man because of the faith of the man and his caring friends!

CRAFTER SUPPLIES

- ☐ Paper plate
- ☐ Tortilla

GROUP SUPPLIES

- ☐ Bowls with margarine and several plastic knives (each chef will use about 1 tbsp.)
- ☐ Shakers with brown sugar (1 per 2 chefs)
- ☐ Shakers with cinnamon (1 per 2 chefs)
- ☐ Wet wipes

TEACHER SUPPLIES

- ☐ Plastic wrap (if you intend to send this craft home)

Mess Management

- You will need several clean salt and pepper type shakers for this activity. Chefs can use plastic spoons to accomplish the same effect; however, the spoons tend to make more of a mess. Shakers can also be made from clean, empty, plastic applesauce or yogurt containers. Poke holes in the bottom of each container with an ice pick or skewer. Fill each container with your ingredients and then cover the top and bottom securely with the lid or aluminum foil.

- This craft can be carefully covered with plastic wrap and sent home with a suggestion to broil the handprint until it is crispy, about four minutes. It can also be eaten as is.

ALLERGY WARNING: *Chefs with wheat allergies could decorate corn tortillas instead.*

Appetizer

Friends help one another. One time some men carried their paralyzed friend to the best healer that they knew: Jesus. What is something nice that a friend has done for you? (gave me a gift, complimented me, invited me over, etc.)

 # Instructions

Get a Buddy:

❶ Today you are going to help a friend. Friends help one another, as the friends of the paralyzed man did.

❷ Look at the person next to you. Ask him his name. Decide whose name comes closest to the letter A. That person will get to print their hand first.

Print Your Hand:

❶ Raise your hand if you are going to print your hand first. I'm going to call you Buddy A.

❷ Buddy A, point to your new friend. Ask him nicely to stand up. Give your new friend a shaker.

❸ Buddy A, spread margarine all over your tortilla.

❹ Place your hand in the center of your tortilla. Spread your fingers.

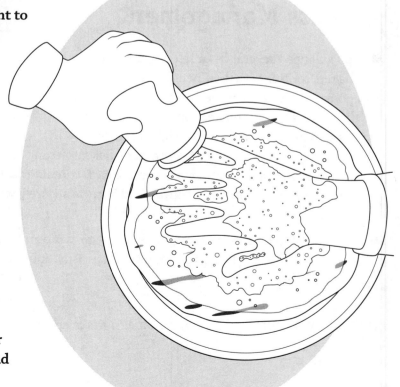

5 New friends, shake, shake, shake all around Buddy A's hand. Cover the tortilla with the cinnamon sugar. It's okay to get some on their hand. Give them about a minute to shake the brown sugar and cinnamon over the tortilla.

6 Okay, Buddy A, lift up your hand. Ask your friend nicely to get you a wet wipe.

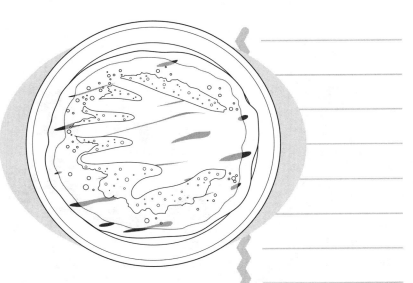

Help Your Friend:

1 Now we are going to switch. Who has been a helper to Buddy A? Now it's the helper's turn to print his or her hand.

2 Buddy A, sit down and take the shaker. Have your new friend spread margarine on his or her tortilla. Then he'll put his hand down on his tortilla.

3 Buddy A, shake, shake, shake all around your friend's hand. Allow about a minute to do this.

4 New friend, lift up your hand. Ask your buddy nicely to get you a wet wipe.

5 Who can see their hand print? Who enjoyed helping a friend?

Dessert

The four friends took the man who couldn't walk to Jesus. He healed the man.

● **How did the four men show they were friends?** (They didn't give up when they couldn't get to Jesus; they made a hole in the roof and let their friend down to Jesus. They trusted Jesus to make their friend well.)

● **What are some things you can do to help your friends?** (Let volunteers share their ideas.)

Dear God, friends are some of the most wonderful gifts You've given us. We should use our hands to help them. Help us see a chance today to help a friend. In Jesus' name we pray, amen.

Fruit Puzzle

Cut some heart puzzles out of fruit.

Bible Basis:
Mark 12:28-34

MEMORY VERSE:
Love your neighbor
as yourself.
Mark 12:31

 ## Bible Snack

Three Jewish groups often scrutinized Jesus: the Herodians, the Pharisees, and the Sadducees. The Herodians were influential Jews who applauded much of the non-Jewish culture around them. The Pharisees were a religious and political party, which valued purity as their scribes interpreted it. They had expounded on the Law of Moses and drawn out hundreds of rituals from it, as many as 613. The Sadducees were at odds with the Pharisees. Many were priests. They believed in the literal translation of the laws and refused to accept the scribes' commentaries on them.

Jesus summarized all of the Old Testament laws with His answer—love. In Mark 12:29 He began by quoting the Shema, "Hear, O Israel: the Lord our God, the Lord is one." This is the Jewish statement of faith recited by the most devout Jews twice a day. Jesus continued by telling His critics that our loving God takes precedence over everything (Deut. 6:5). In loving God, we are able to love those around us. Jesus took the command "Love your neighbor as yourself" out of Leviticus 19:18. His answer was a sermon in itself. Did they love Him as much as they loved themselves?

CRAFTER SUPPLIES

- ☐ Paper plate
- ☐ Plastic knife
- ☐ One fruit slice that is ½" thick, round, and 3" wide

GROUP SUPPLIES

- ☐ 2" or less, heart-shaped cookie cutters (1 per 2 chefs)

TEACHER SUPPLIES

- ☐ Knife
- ☐ Cutting board
- ☐ Large apples or a cantaloupe and 2 kinds of melon

Mess Management

- Wash and cut apples or cantaloupe into half-inch thick slices. They should be wide enough to press a 2" cookie cutter into. Each chef will get one slice. Remove the seeds and place each piece on a separate plate. Cut enough for each chef to have two pieces.

ALLERGY WARNING: *If you have any chefs with allergies to these fruits, use any alternate fruit instead.*

 # Appetizer

What is the most important thing God asks us to do? (Love Him.)
Besides loving God, whom else should we love? (Other people.)

 # Instructions

Cut Fruit Hearts:

❶ Look at the person next to you. You will share a heart cookie cutter. Together, choose one heart cookie cutter.

❷ One of you will go first. Place the cutter in the center of a round fruit slice. Push it all the way down. Carefully pull it out. Give the cookie cutter to your neighbor. Pick out any seeds. Pause while each partner cuts out a heart.

❸ Next, choose two different-colored pieces of melon. Center your cookie cutter and press out two more hearts. Share your cookie cutter with your neighbor. Give your chefs a few minutes to do this.

Divide Your Hearts:

❶ Lay the cut-out fruit hearts on your plate.

❷ Find your knife. Use it to cut each heart in half from top to bottom. Be sure to cut right down the middle of each.

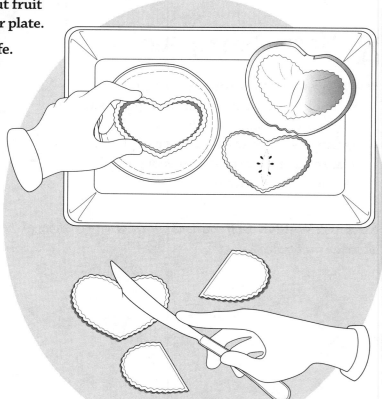

Demonstrate cutting direction. **Who should we love?** (God and others.) **How are you loving your neighbor by sharing right now?**

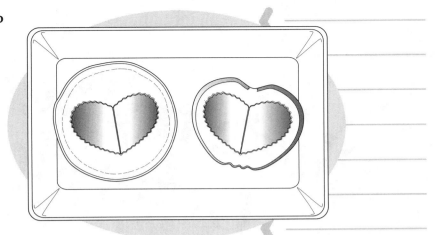

Complete the Puzzle:

❶ Arrange your fruit pieces inside of the fruit puzzles to make colorful, new hearts.

 **Dessert**

Jesus told the man in the crowd that the most important rule is to love God first. Then we are to love others.

● **What are some things you can do to love God with all your heart, soul, mind, and strength?** (Let the children think and tell their ideas. These may include: worship Him with a song, look through His Bible, talk about Him, talk to Him, care for the things and the people that He's made.)

● **What are some ways to love others as yourself?** (they could suggest ways to be kind, thinking about others first, etc.)

Dear God, thank You for loving us so that we can love You and others. Loving everyone all the time is so difficult. Only You can help us to love people. Help us today to love people with our words and our actions. In Jesus' name we pray, amen.

Pleas'n Chees'n Offering

Stamp out some cheesy coins for your offering.

Bible Basis:
Mark 12:41-44

MEMORY VERSE:
Christ is the head of the church.
Ephesians 5:23

 ## Bible Snack

A frequent concept throughout Scripture is God's regard for the state of a person's heart. Is it thankful, like the one healed leper who returned to thank Jesus (Luke 17:11–19)? Is it sincere, like the repentant tax collector who cried out on his knees (Luke 18:9–14)? Is it all consuming, like the woman who washed His feet with expensive perfume (John 12:1–3)? Is it totally trusting, like the widow from this story who tithed her meager finances?

Jesus and His disciples were resting in the inner courtyard of the temple, a place called the Women's Court. Both men and women came here to give their offerings. The money collected was used to pay the temple expenses.

The widow gave two small copper coins or two leptons. These were the smallest and least valuable coins in Palestine, worth only a fraction of a penny in today's economy. The Scripture describes her as "beggarly." Because of her poverty and widow status, the Mosaic Law enabled her to glean the leftovers from the fields and orchards after the day's harvesting had been done. Without a family, she would have had scarce means of providing more than just her daily meals. Jesus was most pleased with her gift, because though her pockets were empty, her heart belonged fully to God.

CRAFTER SUPPLIES

☐ Paper plate

☐ Half a pita, partially opened

☐ Slice of American cheese

☐ Slice of Monterey Jack cheese, about 1/8 inch thick

GROUP SUPPLIES

☐ Small, circular cookie cutters

TEACHER SUPPLIES

☐ Knife

☐ Cutting board

☐ Plastic wrap (if you intend to send the pitas home)

Mess Management

● Cut the Monterey Jack cheese slices from a block of cheese. Each slice should measure about 2" x 4".

● Cut the pitas in half so that each chef will have one pocket. Partially open each half.

● These cheesy pitas can be sent home to be baked, or your chefs can snack on them cold.

ALLERGY WARNING: *If you have any chefs who are allergic to milk, soy cheese can be substituted. If any of your chefs have a wheat allergy, they can place their cheese coins in folded paper plates or corn tortillas.*

 **Appetizer**

Name some things that belong to God. (the church, nature, our families, money, etc.) **What does God do with the things that belong to Him?** (He shares them, He lets us use and enjoy them.)

 **Instructions**

Cut Your Coins:

❶ Use the cookie cutters to cut shapes out of your cheese slices. Cut as many as you can. These are cheese coins.

❷ Set aside the leftover cheese.

❸ When we give money to God, what might it be used for? (helping people, giving offerings, helping friends, etc.)

Fill Your Wallet:

❶ Carefully open your pita a little bit. Be careful to not rip it. This is your wallet.

❷ Place your cheese coins inside.

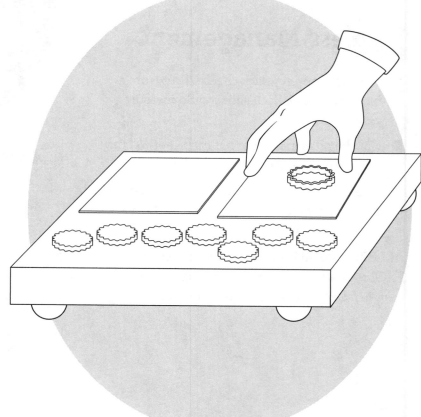

 ## Dessert

● **Why did Jesus say the woman gave more than all the rich people?** (She gave all that she had. The rich gave only part of their money.)

● **Why do God's people give their offerings?** (To show God we love Him; to help the church do God's work.)

Dear God, You own everything. Thank You for giving us everything we have. Help us cheerfully give back some of what You've given us. In Jesus' name we pray, amen.

Hot Dog! It's Jesus' Birthday!

Re-create elements of the Bethlehem scene with a hot dog snack!

Bible Basis: Luke 2:1–7

MEMORY VERSE: God sent his Son. Galatians 4:4

 Bible Snack

God planned Jesus' coming for hundreds of years prior to His birth. Micah 5:2, written about 700 years before Christ's birth, foretold that Bethlehem would be the Messiah's birthplace. Bethlehem was also called the "town of David" because it had been King David's hometown. Both Joseph and Mary were David's descendants. Isaiah 11:1 prophesied that Jesus' lineage would be from David's line.

When the Roman emperor Augustus wanted to count the number of people living in the Roman territory, he ordered all families to return to the town of their ancestry. This was to help him determine how many people should be paying taxes and who could serve in his army. The Jews would have had to pay taxes, but they were exempt from serving in the Roman military. Mary and Joseph set out on the 70-mile journey to Bethlehem. It is likely that they sought out a place to stay with their Davidic kin there.

Inns in those times were typically guest rooms built onto houses. Since there was no room available for Mary and Joseph, they were permitted to stay in a dark and dirty stable. This was very possibly a cave. The manger used for the crib was an animal feed box. It might have been a trough carved into a rock wall, or it could have been built of stone and mud cement, or of clay and straw. It seems God saved no luxuries for Himself when He came to earth.

CRAFTER SUPPLIES

- [ ] Half a hot dog bun
- [ ] 1 cooked, bun-size hot dog, cut by the teacher
- [ ] Toothpick
- [ ] Plastic knife
- [ ] Quartered American or Colby-Jack cheese slice

GROUP SUPPLIES

- [ ] Bowl of shredded cheddar cheese, about 2 tbsp. per chef
- [ ] Bowl of mustard or ketchup with several toothpicks

TEACHER SUPPLIES

- [ ] Knife
- [ ] Cutting board
- [ ] Scissors

Mess Management

- Cook hot dogs and chill before using.

- Prepare the bowls of cheddar cheese and mustard or ketchup.

- Prepare the hot dog buns by cutting horizontally so they will fold up.

- Cut the American or Colby-Jack cheese slices in quarters. Clean scissors are the quickest way to do this. If you leave the wrapper on, the cheese will stay fresh longer.

- If you have a class of more than five chefs, you might want to simplify this activity by slicing the hot dogs yourself. Otherwise, seat your chefs around you at a table so you can better monitor how they cut their hot dogs.

ALLERGY WARNING: *If any chefs are allergic to milk, you can substitute soy cheese for the donkey's blanket. If any chefs have allergies to hot dogs, they can use a piece of rolled up turkey or ham.*

 **Appetizer**

Jesus was not born in a hospital. He wasn't even born in a house, because there was no room for His family. Where was He born? (a stable.) **What special bed was Jesus laid in?** (a manger, a feeding trough for farm animals.)

 **Instructions**

Slice the Donkey Pieces:

Complete this step with small classes of five or fewer. Otherwise you might want to cut the hot dog pieces ahead of time and go to step two.

❶ **Cut a small piece of hot dog off one end. This is the donkey's head.**

❷ **You have a big hot dog piece left. Cut this in half. These are the donkey's legs.**

❸ **Take a hot dog half and cut into it about halfway. Do the same to the other hotdog half. These are the donkey's four legs.** Demonstrate this step.

Create the Donkey:

❶ **Put your three hot dog pieces together. First, lay the little head on the table. Next to it lay down the body pieces. Are the legs together?** Demonstrate this.

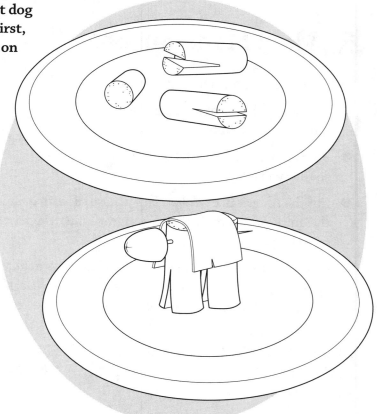

❷ Push the toothpick through the body pieces and then through the head. Leave a little toothpick sticking out for the tail. Demonstrate this.

❸ Stand up your donkey. Lay the cheese slice across the donkey's back. This is a blanket.

❹ Stick your toothpick in the mustard or ketchup. Add two little mustard or ketchup eyes to your donkey.

Make the Manger:

❶ Put a spoonful of cheese into a hotdog bun. This is the manger.

🧁 Dessert

● **What happened during the night that Mary and Joseph stayed in the stable?** (Jesus was born.)

● **What are some ways you can celebrate Jesus' birth?** (Let children volunteer answers.)

Dear God, we love to celebrate the birth of Your Son, Jesus! You sent Him to love us and to show us how to love You back. What a wonderful gift! In Jesus' name we pray, amen.

Christ Child Crown

String together a miniature candy crown.

Bible Basis:
Luke 2:21-38

MEMORY VERSE:
God sent his Son.
Galatians 4:4

 ## Bible Snack

The Law of Moses had rituals tied to the birth of a child. After eight days a boy was to be circumcised. Another 32 days passed before his mother could enter the temple. Keeping disease, human blood, and dirt from entering the temple helped set it apart in the minds of the people. The outer cleanliness represented what God desired for people's inner hearts. A lamb was then offered for the mother's purification, or if she was poor, as Jesus' parents were, a pair of turtledoves or young pigeons would suffice.

If the baby was a firstborn boy, five shekels of silver also had to be paid (Num. 18:16). This money was given to redeem the baby from his special service in the temple (Exod. 13:2). When the tribe of Levi was assigned this task, firstborn sons were no longer needed to serve. However, the priests continued to require the payment of this money.

Little did Mary and Joseph understand, their son was God's temple. He would live a life of supreme service to His Father God. He would be the eternal High Priest; no other would ever need to intercede between sinful people and their holy God.

CRAFTER SUPPLIES

- ☐ Pull-apart licorice piece separated as specified in MESS MANAGEMENT
- ☐ One 3" fruit leather strip
- ☐ Round candy with a hole in the middle
- ☐ Paper plate

GROUP SUPPLIES

- ☐ None

TEACHER SUPPLIES

- ☐ Scissors

Mess Management

- For each chef, separate one pull-apart licorice into two pieces. One piece should have two licorice strands in it. The other, thicker piece will have the rest of the licorice strands.

- Cut a 3" strip of fruit leather for each chef.

ALLERGY WARNING: *If you have any chefs who are allergic to peanuts, handling the fruit leather, licorice, or a candy might be dangerous. Instead, they could use string cheese in place of the licorice, with a slice of American cheese replacing the fruit leather, and a thin slice of apple with a hole cut in the middle instead of the candy.*

 **Appetizer**

Jesus was born a king, the very Son of God. He didn't look like a king though. **What types of things are part of a king's royal outfit?** (crown, throne, robe, etc.)

 Instructions

String the Gem:

❶ Take the skinny licorice piece. String the round candy onto it.

❷ Push the round candy to the middle of the licorice string. This is a gem on the special crown you're making.

❸ Tie a knot around the licorice. Demonstrate this. Some chefs will have trouble tying, so you may need to help.

Make the Crown:

❶ Take your thick licorice strand. Lay it in a circle shape on your plate.

❷ Bend your thin licorice strand into a circle. Lay it on top of the thicker circle. Line up the end pieces.

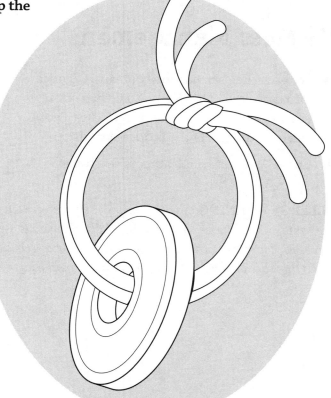

Tape the Strands:

❶ Take your fruit leather piece. Use it like tape. Tape around the ends of the licorice to make the circle crown complete.

 Dessert

- **What happened when Mary and Joseph took Jesus to the temple?** (Simeon and Anna recognized Jesus as God's Son.)

- **How did Simeon and Anna know that Jesus was God's Son?** (God helped both Simeon and Anna know that Mary's baby was God's Son.)

Dear Jesus, we praise You for being God's Son. Thank You for loving us enough to leave Your wonderful heaven and come to our sinful earth. In Jesus' name we pray, amen.

Blooming Beauty

Plant a flavorful flower in some delicious dirt.

Bible Basis:
Luke 2:40-52;
Matthew
13:55-56

MEMORY VERSE:
[Jesus] grew and
became strong.
Luke 2:40

Bible Snack

The law given in Deuteronomy required that the Israelites celebrate the Passover and the Festival of Unleavened Bread each year (Deut. 16:1–8). Jesus' family traveled to Jerusalem to take part in the festivities there. After a week of celebrating, they began the long trip home in the company of friends and other travelers. Traveling in groups protected everyone from robbers. Women and children led the way, while the men guarded the rear of the caravan. At 12 years old, Jesus was nearly an adult. He could have joined either part of the group and thus easily been overlooked by his parents.

The temple courts were a place of learning. During Passover, rabbis would have gathered to teach and debate truths. Jewish scholars were expecting the Messiah, and so the Savior's coming could have been discussed. The rabbis Jesus spoke with in the temple were amazed that such a young boy could understand Scripture so deeply.

The Bible doesn't give details about Jesus' education. However, most Jews during that time were taught to read and write. If Jesus had been trained to become a rabbi, He would have begun lessons in Leviticus as early as five years old. Memorizing the text would have been the focus of His schooling. However, He would not have been expected to join in theological discussions until the age of 15. His youth wasn't the whole of their amazement; it appears He spent several days engrossed in their discussions.

CRAFTER SUPPLIES

- ☐ Ice-cream cone
- ☐ Half a big pretzel rod
- ☐ One 4" fruit leather strip
- ☐ One 8" fruit leather strip
- ☐ Plastic knife

GROUP SUPPLIES

- ☐ Chocolate pudding with several spoons

TEACHER SUPPLIES

- ☐ Milk
- ☐ Chocolate pudding mix
- ☐ Spoon
- ☐ Bowl
- ☐ Spatula

Mess Management

- Cut the fruit leather as specified in CRAFTER SUPPLIES.

- Break the big pretzels in half, so there is one half per chef.

- Prepare the chocolate pudding and refrigerate it until it is needed.

ALLERGY WARNING: *If you have any chefs who are allergic to milk, nondairy whipped cream can be substituted for the chocolate pudding. You could add some dairy-free chocolate cookies to it to give it the appearance of dirt.*

 # Appetizer

Jesus grew and learned just like you and me. He was a baby, then He grew into a child, and then became an adult. What things help you grow? (good food, books, sleep, school, etc.)

 # Instructions

Fill the Flower Pot:

❶ Carefully put four spoonfuls of pudding in your ice-cream cone pot. This is your dirt.

❷ Dirt is full of good things that help plants grow. Jesus grew from a little baby to a man. What kinds of things helped Jesus grow? (food, His parents' love, listening to the Scriptures, talking to God, etc.)

Make the Bloom:

❶ Lay the end of your pretzel on the end of your little fruit strip.

❷ Roll the fruit strip around the pretzel end. This is the center of your flower.

❸ Find your long fruit strip. Slice it into several squares. Can you make about six ?

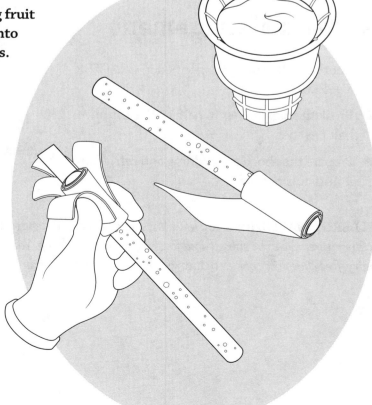

④ Take one fruit strip square. This is a petal. Stick the bottom of it on the center of your flower. It should hang over like a petal.
Demonstrate this step.

⑤ Make more petals. Stick the other fruit leather squares around the top of your pretzel to finish making the petals.

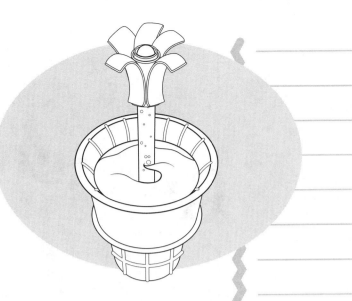

Plant the Flower:

❶ Carefully push your pretzel flower stem down into your dirt until it stands tall. Some students might need help pushing their flower down into the grooves at the bottom of their ice-cream cones.

 Dessert

● **Why was Jesus still at the temple?** (He wanted to be in His heavenly Father's house. He wanted to become more wise. He wanted to talk with the temple teachers.)

● **How can we keep learning more about God?** (read and listen to Bible stories, pray, etc.)

Dear God, thank You for filling our lives with things that help us grow. You have given us so much! Like Jesus, we want to grow into wiser, kinder, and more loving people. In Jesus' name we pray, amen.

Go Fish!

Decorate your own fruity fish.

Bible Basis:
Luke 5:1–11;
Matthew 4:18–22

MEMORY VERSE:
[Jesus] grew and became strong.
Luke 2:40

 ## Bible Snack

The Sea of Galilee was a large lake, 13 miles long and eight miles wide. Nine cities and about 30 fishing towns surrounded it. At least seven of Jesus' disciples were fishermen. Two had been John the Baptist's disciples the year prior to this story (John 1:35–42). All of them were familiar with Jesus' teaching and miracles. This was typical. A rabbi would spend time with specific men before he extended them the honor of becoming his disciples.

Fishing was a strenuous profession. It was done with lines and hooks, harpoons and nets. Fishermen who used nets and boats had to deal with frequent, sudden storms and spent time on land mending and cleaning nets. Sometimes they worked long hours and caught nothing.

Adding to the miracle of this story is that Jesus was not a fisherman. He sent the fishermen back out to make a catch during a time of day when the fish would have been in deeper waters and thus not near the nets. Yet, Jesus' advice was overwhelmingly good. The fishermen who obeyed Him were astounded that He could have such power over the details of their everyday lives.

CRAFTER SUPPLIES

☐ Bowl

☐ 5 oz. paper cup filled with: 2 grape halves, a red candy sprinkle, and 3 thin apples slices, about 2 mm thick (see MESS MANAGEMENT for how to cut these)

GROUP SUPPLIES

☐ Several bowls of blueberry pie filling or blue gelatin, with several plastic spoons (prepare a 1 c. bowl per 4 students)

TEACHER SUPPLIES

☐ Knife

☐ Cutting board

☐ Canned pears (a 15 oz. can contains from 4–8 pear halves)

🧴 Mess Management

- Cut one grape in half for each chef.

- Prepare the gelatin or dish out the blueberry pie filling.

- Prepare one 5 oz. paper cup per chef as specified in CRAFTER SUPPLIES.

- Wash and slice an apple into approximately one millimeter slices. For each chef, cut two triangular pieces (you will make two triangles by halving an apple slice, but you'll need only one) and two crescents (refer to the illustration on the following page). If you cut the apples ahead of time, soak them in a solution of 1 tbsp. lemon juice and a quart of water.

ALLERGY WARNING: *If you have any chefs who are allergic to peanuts, they may react to the candy. If they do, you can use the tip of a baby carrot instead.*

 # Appetizer

Some of Jesus' best friends were fishermen. Have you ever been fishing or watched someone fish? Was it easy to catch a fish?

 # Instructions

Make the Sea:

❶ Carefully put two spoonfuls of blueberry pie filling (or gelatin) into your bowl. This is the sea.

❷ Once you've finished, raise your hand. I will place a fish in your sea.
Distribute the pear halves. Place them flat side down, one in each chef's bowl.

Create the Fish:

❶ Look inside your paper cup. You should have two grape halves and three apple pieces. One piece is a triangle and two are part circles.

❷ Take out one part circle apple piece. Hold it up. This is the tail fin. Place this on the sea near the small end of your fish.
Demonstrate this step.

❸ Take out the other part circle of apple.

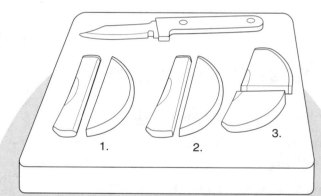

Break it in half. These are the side fins. Hold each side fin so the peel faces up. Push these down into the sides of your fish. Demonstrate this step.

❹ Find your last apple piece, the triangle. This is the dorsal fin. It goes on top. Push it down into the middle of your pear.

❺ Add the two grape eyes and the candy sprinkle for the mouth.

 # Dessert

● **What did the four fishermen do when Jesus told them, "Follow Me"?** (They left their fishing nets and boats to follow Jesus as His disciples.)

● **How do you think we can follow Jesus?** (Let the children discuss this. They might talk about doing what is right, learning from the Bible, etc.)

Dear Jesus, thank You for asking us to follow You. Please show us how to follow You. In Jesus' name we pray, amen.

White as Snowballs

Coat a handmade cookie with sweet snow.

Bible Basis:
Luke 7:36-50

MEMORY VERSE:
[Jesus] went around
doing good.
Acts 10:38

 ## Bible Snack

Jesus' love for humankind drew people to Him. People sought out His forgiveness because they knew He was so willing to give it. People trapped in sin would have been extended no love or encouragement to repent from religious leaders. They were untouchable. Rabbis and Pharisees would have nothing to do with notorious sinners. The word *Pharisee* actually means "separated one." Known sinners would not have been allowed in the temple.

It's unclear why Simon didn't extend the ordinary hospitality to Jesus. He was hosting a large party. However, Jesus was surely one of his guests of honor. Jesus did not get His feet washed, His head anointed with oil, or even receive a kiss of greeting from His host. Instead, a woman with a reputation for immorality extended all of these to Him. She was not invited. It was not unusual, though, for uninvited guests to come to large parties.

Because Jesus would have reclined to eat, she would have been able to touch His feet without approaching the table or speaking with Him. If Jesus had spoken with her, He would have committed yet another faux pas. Rabbis were not supposed to address women in public, especially immoral women. Simon was appalled that this unclean woman was touching Jesus' feet and anointing Him with ointment that he suspected had been bought with immoral earnings. He couldn't grasp that a righteous man, needless to say, a righteous God, could tolerate a sinner.

CRAFTER SUPPLIES

☐ Bowl

☐ Plastic spoon

☐ Zip-top sandwich bag filled with: ½ graham cracker, 1 tbsp. chocolate chips, 3 little stick pretzels

GROUP SUPPLIES

☐ Marshmallow cream (about 2 tbsp. per chef)

☐ Bowl of shredded coconut (about 2 tbsp. per chef)

TEACHER SUPPLIES

☐ Cooking spray

Mess Management

● Fill one zip-top sandwich bag per chef as specified in CRAFTER SUPPLIES.

● Prepare the bowls of marshmallow cream and shredded coconut.

ALLERGY WARNING: *If you have a chef who is allergic to peanuts, handling the candy or coconut could be dangerous. Allow him to roll his ball in more crushed graham crackers. If you have a chef who is allergic to wheat products, you can use rice cereal in the mix instead.*

 **Appetizer**

Have you ever done anything to hurt someone? Have you ever not done something kind that you should have? God calls these things sin. When God forgives our sins, He makes our sinful hearts clean—like snow!

 Instructions

Crush the Sin:

❶ Hold up a zip-top bag filled as specified in CRAFTER SUPPLIES. **This bag of goodies is like sin. Sometimes sin seems good. Sometimes sin looks good. Is sin good?** (No.)

❷ No, sin is bad. It's dirty. It always hurts you. It hurts others. **Go ahead and squish up your bag. Squeeze it. Crush what's inside.** Demonstrate how to press the bag down onto the table and crush the pieces inside.

Spoon in God's Love:

❶ **Add two spoonfuls of white, clean marshmallow cream to your bowl. This is like God's love.**

❷ **Carefully pour your bag that's like sin into your bowl. Use your spoon to mix it into the cream. God's love comes into our sinful lives. He forgives you and me. He helps to undo the hurt our sins have caused.**

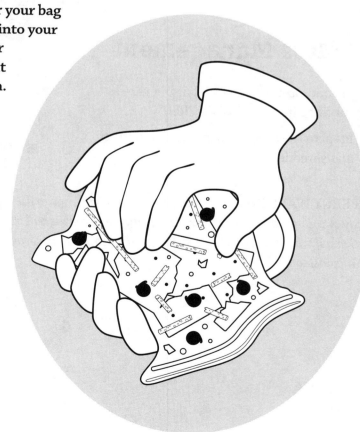

God's Love Covers All:

❶ When your spoon can no longer mix well, raise your hand. I will come around and put cooking spray on your palms. Then you can squish the mixture into a ball. It is okay if some small pieces come off. Spray each chef's palms when his or her mixture becomes stiff.

❷ Roll your ball in the coconut. Once it's covered, place it in your bowl. The coconut is like God's love—it covers our sins!

 # Dessert

● **Why did the woman show so much love to Jesus?** (She knew Jesus had forgiven her.)

● **Why does Jesus forgive us our sins?** (He loves us. When we are sorry for our sins and want to be forgiven, Jesus forgives us.)

Dear God, thank You for loving us all the time! It's so easy for us to be unkind, unloving, and selfish. Thank You for forgiving us when we ask You. Thank You for helping to undo the hurt we've caused. You are such a good God! In Jesus' name we pray, amen.

Bling Bling Ring

Turn an ice-cream cone into a colorful lesson in prayer.

Bible Basis:
Luke 11:1–4

MEMORY VERSE:
We know and rely on the love God has for us. 1 John 4:16

Bible Snack

Jesus was an expert at prayer. He practiced it often. Because Jesus was the ultimate authority on how to approach the Father, we should take His example of prayer to heart.

The "Lord's Prayer," as this passage is called, is Jesus' most definitive lesson on how to pray. We can glean several important things from it. First, this prayer is not repetitive or wordy. Jesus told His disciples that babbling in prayer was something pagans did (Matt. 6:7). Instead, prayer should be filled with meaningful words.

Jesus begins with addressing God as *Abba,* the Aramaic word for "daddy." Jesus wants us to approach God reverently, but with the understanding that His Father is personal and loving. Jesus then praises His Father. The use of the words may "your kingdom come" and may "your will be done" (Matt. 6:10) are reminders to us of the right perspective—that acknowledging God's way is best.

Next Jesus teaches us to present our needs. The Bible says that God already knows our needs (Matt. 6:8); requesting them is a reminder to ourselves that God is the one who meets our every need. Then Jesus points out that giving and receiving forgiveness go hand in hand. Lastly, Jesus shows us that we should request God's help to avoid evil and not be harmed by it.

CRAFTER SUPPLIES

- ☐ Paper plate
- ☐ Plastic knife or craft stick
- ☐ Top half of an ice-cream cone

GROUP SUPPLIES

- ☐ White icing
- ☐ Various gem-sized candies: yellow, green, white, and red

TEACHER SUPPLIES

- ☐ Serrated knife
- ☐ Food dye

Mess Management

- ● Use a serrated knife to separate the top of an ice-cream cone from the bottom. The ring on the top is what each chef needs.

- ● Use the food dye to color the icing. Create a color that will contrast with the candy gems, such as orange, blue, purple, etc.

- ● Prepare a bowl of candy as described in GROUP SUPPLIES.

ALLERGY WARNING: *If you have a chef who is allergic to peanuts, handling the candy could be dangerous. Allow her to decorate with raisins instead. If you have a chef who is allergic to wheat products, you can use fruit leather instead of the cone.*

 **Appetizer**

Jesus talked to His Father often. He taught us how to pray in the Lord's Prayer. What kinds of things can we talk to God about? (feelings, problems, needs, family, anything, etc.)

 Instructions

Ice the Ring:

❶ Use your plastic knife or craft stick to spread the icing on the outside of your ice-cream cone ring.

❷ Set the ring on your plate.

Add the Prayer Gems:

❶ I'm going to read you a poem about prayer. Get your hands ready to help me.

Read the poem aloud, and act it out as directed below.

Yellow is for sunny praise. God is great in so many ways.
Raise your hands in praise.

Green is for our growing needs, like food, clothes, and doing good deeds.
Use your hand to demonstrate eating, pointing to your clothes, and sharing.

White is for a clean, clean start. When I forgive others, God cleans my heart.

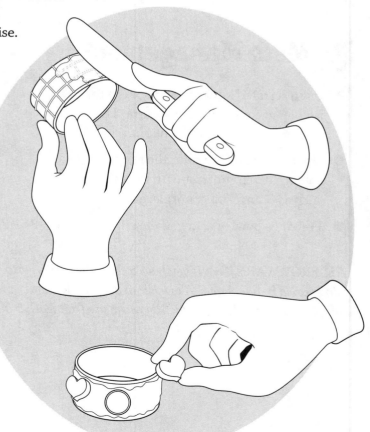

Use your hands to hug someone and then place your hands over your heart.

Red is my call for help. Stop me from hurting others or myself.
Put your palm out flat like a traffic cop.

❷ **Good. Now I'll read this prayer poem again. You line up your colors in the order I read them.** Reread the poem slowly.

❸ **Let's review the colors. What is yellow?** (Praising God.) **Next is green. What does green stand for?** (Talking to God about what we need.) **Then comes white. You need two whites. Why?** (We need to forgive other people, and God can forgive us.) **Last you should have red. What is red?** (Asking for God's help to not sin.)

❹ **Stick your candy gems on your prayer ring.**

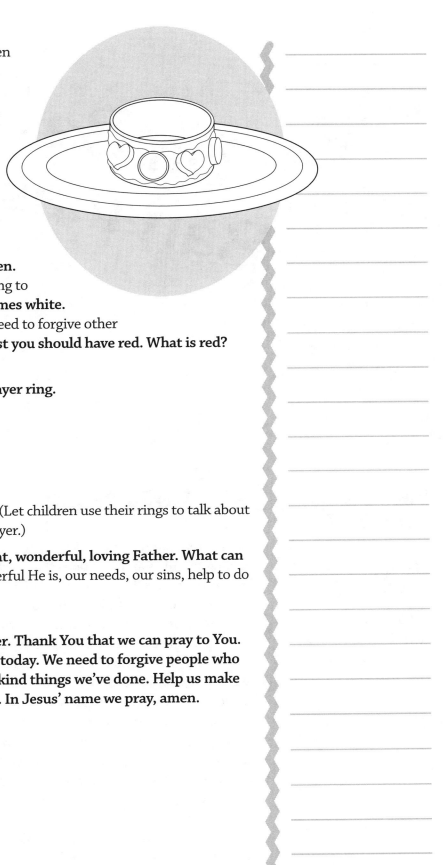

 ## Dessert

● **How does Jesus teach us to pray?** (Let children use their rings to talk about the different parts of the Lord's Prayer.)

● **We can talk to God like He's a great, wonderful, loving Father. What can we talk to God about?** (how wonderful He is, our needs, our sins, help to do the right thing, etc.)

Dear God, You are our heavenly Father. Thank You that we can pray to You. We know You'll give us what we need today. We need to forgive people who have hurt us. Please forgive us for unkind things we've done. Help us make choices to be kind to those around us. In Jesus' name we pray, amen.

Ba Ba Bananas

Assemble a sweet sheep banana treat.

Bible Basis:
Luke 15:1-7

MEMORY VERSE:
[Jesus] went around
doing good.
Acts 10:38

 ## Bible Snack

The Pharisees and teachers Jesus often criticized were more concerned with holding to rituals and traditions than with loving. Most went far beyond the laws given in the Old Testament to maintain "cleanliness." Jesus, on the other hand, was motivated by love. He touched lepers. He ate with tax collectors. He let prostitutes wash His feet with perfume.

Sheep were common animals during Jesus' time. They were also valuable assets. They were raised for food, used as sacrifices in worship, skinned for making jackets, and counted as a measure of wealth.

Jesus draws many comparisons between sheep and His followers. Both are familiar with the voice of their shepherd. Sheep, like people, are social animals, herding together, often mindlessly following one another. Both are also predisposed to wander off. A shepherd often had to search for a lost sheep. A good shepherd would never wait for his lost sheep to wander back to the fold.

Likewise, God pursues people who have strayed. Jesus used the story of the lost sheep to demonstrate God's love for sinful people. The other two parables—the lost coin and the prodigal son—both convey that God's love for people, those sinful or faithful, is abundant.

CRAFTER SUPPLIES

- ☐ 2" banana piece
- ☐ Paper plate
- ☐ 5 oz. paper cup with:
  2 mini chocolate chips,
  3 mini marshmallows, a
  plastic spoon, and a pink
  candy sprinkle

GROUP SUPPLIES

- ☐ Bowl with ¼ c. caramel
  (1 per 2 chefs)
- ☐ Bowl of ¼ c. coconut (1
  per 2 chefs)
- ☐ Wet wipes

TEACHER SUPPLIES

- ☐ Knife
- ☐ Cutting board

Mess Management

- Honey can be substituted for caramel; however, the toppings tend to slide a bit more easily with the honey.

- Prepare a paper cup for each chef as specified in CRAFTER SUPPLIES.

- Leave the peels on the bananas when you cut them. Slice a 2" banana piece per chef.

- Prepare a bowl of ¼ c. honey/caramel per two chefs.

- Prepare a bowl of ¼ c. coconut per two chefs.

ALLERGY WARNING: *If you have a chef who is allergic to peanuts, the candy and coconut can be dangerous for him to touch. A cooked hot dog or a rolled-up slice of ham or turkey could be coated with mayonnaise and rolled in shredded mozzarella instead.*

 # Appetizer

What kind of animal does a shepherd take care of? (Sheep.) **How are people like sheep?** (Both wander away at times from the person caring for them.) **Jesus says we are like sheep. If we wander away from His love and care, He will find us and bring us back.**

 # Instructions

Make the Ba Ba Body:

❶ **Peel your banana piece. This is your sheep.** Some chefs may need help.

❷ **Roll your banana around in the caramel.** This will be messy.

❸ **Place your sticky banana in the bowl of coconut. Push it around until it is covered. Now your sheep has wool!**

❹ **Set your woolly banana sheep on your plate.**

Assemble the Face and Tail:

❶ **Look in your paper cup. Find your mini chocolate chips. These are the sheep's eyes. Push the pointed side of the chocolate chips into one end of your banana.**

❷ Find two mini marshmallows. These are the sheep's ears. Dip each one in the caramel. Set these over the eyes, on top of the banana.

❸ Find the pink candy sprinkle. This is the sheep's mouth. Dip it in caramel. Stick it under the chocolate chip eyes.

❹ Take your last marshmallow. This is the sheep's tail. Dip it in caramel and stick it on the back end of the **banana.** Children will probably need wet wipes after completing their sheep.

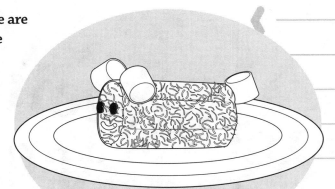

 # Dessert

● **Why did the shepherd go look for the lost sheep?** (The shepherd loved the lost sheep. He loved all his sheep.)

● **Why did Jesus tell this story?** (He wanted to help us learn that He loves us.)

Dear Jesus, You are such a good shepherd. Thank You for loving us. We don't ever want to be lost sheep who are far away from You. In Jesus' name we pray, amen.

Resurrection Sunrise

Make a plate full of sunshine with tropical fruit.

Bible Basis:
Luke 23:46–24:12;
1 Corinthians 15:4-5

MEMORY VERSE:
Jesus Christ is the same yesterday and today and forever.
Hebrews 13:8

 ## Bible Snack

When Jesus died, the sky darkened, the curtain in the temple split, the earth shook, and tombs opened (Matt 27:45–53). Two secret followers of Jesus—Joseph of Arimathea and Nicodemus—took His body to be buried (John 19:38–39). Joseph and Nicodemus were members of the Sanhedrin, the Jewish high council. Joseph may not have been present to cast his vote when the Sanhedrin unanimously condemned Jesus. Nicodemus was a sympathetic follower (John 7:51). They risked their reputations when they asked Pilate for Jesus' body.

As was customary, Joseph and Nicodemus wrapped Jesus' body in linens with 75 pounds of myrrh and aloe (John 19:39). They then laid Him in a new tomb, an honorary place to be buried; most people were laid in shallow graves. This tomb was probably carved in a limestone cave commonly found around the hills of Jerusalem. A stone was rolled over the entrance, and Roman military stood guard to prevent Jesus' followers from stealing the body.

Jesus' death occurred right before the yearly Passover celebration. During the first Passover, the blood of a lamb spread over the doorposts of a home preserved the life of its firstborn son. It is interesting to note that during the Jewish Passover Seder, a piece of pierced matzah is broken, wrapped, and hidden. At the end of the meal the matzah is found. Jewish Christians today believe that this Jewish tradition, established years before Jesus' coming, represents our Bread of Life, pierced, killed, buried, and raised from the dead. Jesus IS the Passover lamb!

CRAFTER SUPPLIES
- ☐ Paper plate

GROUP SUPPLIES
- ☐ Vanilla yogurt with several spoons (2 tbsp. per chef)
- ☐ Bowl of mandarin orange slices (6 pieces per chef)

TEACHER SUPPLIES
- ☐ Pineapple rings (1 per chef)
- ☐ Plastic fork

Mess Management

● Prepare the bowls of yogurt and mandarin orange slices. Put several plastic spoons in each.

ALLERGY WARNING: *If you have a chef who is allergic to milk products, use nondairy whipped topping instead of yogurt. If you have a chef who is allergic to citrus, you can use apple slices rather than mandarin oranges.*

 # Appetizer

Who has seen a sunset? What always happens after the night is over? (The sun rises.) **The women went at sunrise to Jesus' tomb. But they found that He was alive! We can believe that Jesus is alive.**

 # Instructions

Make the Sun:

❶ Put a spoonful of mandarin orange slices on your plate. Count them. You need about six.

❷ While your chefs are counting, place one pineapple ring on each of their plates. **What do you think this pineapple ring looks like?** (The sun.)

❸ Lay the oranges around your pineapple sun. These are the sun's rays.

Spoon the Dip:

❶ Carefully place a spoonful of yogurt in the center of your pineapple sunrise.

 **Dessert**

- **What happened when the women went to the tomb at sunrise?** (The stone was rolled away. Two angels told them that Jesus is alive.)
- **What can we believe about Jesus?** (Jesus is alive!)

Dear Jesus, You died and were buried, but You rose again, just like the sun! Thank You for that. When we see the sun, we will remember that You are alive! In Jesus' name we pray, amen.

Sweet Scepter

This pretzel is scrumptious enough for a King!

**Bible Basis:
John 1:35-42;
Matthew
16:13-17**

*MEMORY VERSE:
Jesus Christ is the
same yesterday and
today and forever.
Hebrews 13:8*

Bible Snack

Throughout the New Testament, Jesus is referred to as God's Son. Gabriel, the angel, announced it to Mary (Luke 1:32). Elizabeth, Mary's cousin, affirmed it (Luke 1:43). At Jesus' birth, an angel publicized it among the shepherds (Luke 2:11). Righteous Simeon revealed it at the temple (Luke 2:28–32). Anna, the prophetess, praised God for it (Luke 2:38). John the Baptist, Jesus' cousin, testified to it (John 1:32–34). The Holy Spirit declared it at Jesus' baptism (Luke 3:22). One by one the apostles realized it. Saul was revolutionized by it (Acts 9:3–6). Then he wholeheartedly dedicated his life to preaching this good news to the known world.

Some people believed that Jesus was John the Baptist reincarnated (Matt. 14:1–2) after his beheading by Herod. Others thought Jesus was the prophet Elijah whom they expected to return (Mal. 4:5). Simon Peter had known Jesus for several years when Jesus asked him, "Who do you say I am?" Peter's answer came from divine revelation: "You are the Christ, the Son of the living God."

CRAFTER SUPPLIES

- ☐ Paper plate
- ☐ 1 pretzel rod
- ☐ 1 large marshmallow

GROUP SUPPLIES

- ☐ Bowls of marshmallow cream with several plastic knives or craft sticks (¼ c. per 4 chefs)
- ☐ Bowls of sprinkles (⅛ c. per 4 chefs)

TEACHER SUPPLIES

Mess Management

- Prepare the bowls of marshmallow cream. One ¼ c. bowl can serve about four chefs. Place two plastic knives or craft sticks in each bowl, one per two chefs.

- Prepare the bowls of sprinkles.

- Be sure the marshmallow cream is room temperature. Otherwise, it is difficult to spread.

ALLERGY WARNING: *If you have a chef who is allergic to peanuts, handling the candy could be dangerous. Allow him to roll his marshmallow in crushed rice cereal. If you have a chef who is allergic to wheat products, you can use a carrot instead of the pretzel. Use cream cheese to attach the marshmallow on the end.*

 # Appetizer

How could you tell a king from a regular person? What things do we think a king would wear? (jeweled crown, purple robe, scepter, etc.) **People never saw Jesus wear a beautiful crown, royal clothes, or hold a scepter. But He is the King of kings—God's Son. That's why we're going to make a scepter like a king would hold.**

 # Instructions

Attach the Ornament:

❶ Push the end of the pretzel rod into the middle of the marshmallow. Twist it down so that the marshmallow stays.

Add the Jewels:

❶ Use a plastic knife or craft stick to paint marshmallow cream all over your marshmallow.

❷ Roll the sticky marshmallow in sprinkles.

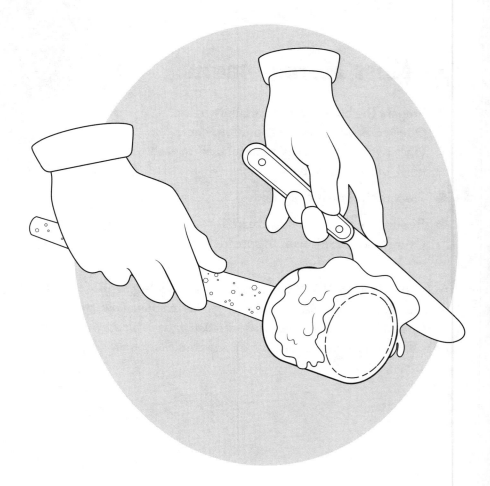

 # Dessert

- **What did Peter say when Jesus asked, "Who am I?"** (Peter said, "You are Jesus, God's Son.")

- **How do you think we can know Jesus is God's Son?** (Reinforce that God can use many different ways to help us know that Jesus is His Son: reading the Bible, listening to Bible stories, talking with people who know Jesus, praying, etc.)

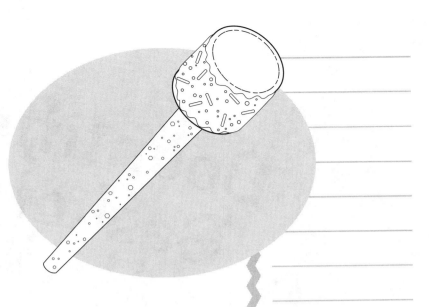

Dear Jesus, You are the King of kings—God's Son! The more we talk to You and listen to Your words from the Bible, the better we get to know You. In Jesus' name we pray, amen.

Bountiful Basket

Craft a fruit-flavored basket and fill it with bread and fish.

**Bible Basis:
John 6:5-13**

*MEMORY VERSE:
A friend loves at all times.
Proverbs 17:17*

 ## Bible Snack

It was nearly Passover. Crowds of Jewish people flocked to Jesus, having heard about His miracles. About 5,000 men were in the crowd following Jesus. This number doesn't include women and children who were there. Jesus Himself was avoiding certain cities because there had been a plot to kill Him (John 5:1, 18). Exactly one more year would pass before His death and resurrection.

Philip was a local to this area. His hometown was Bethsaida. Choosing to ask Philip where to find food made sense. However, in doing so, Jesus was emphasizing the impossibility of the task. Philip calculated it would cost eight months' wages to pay for everyone's meal (John 6:7).

The picnic the boy brought the disciples was a poor man's meal. Barley was the staple bread for the impoverished. The two fish were the size of sardines. In spite of the meager portions, the crowd was fed. The customary practice was to collect leftover bread at the end of a meal; Jews believed all bread was a gift from God. The 12 baskets of leftovers collected at the end made Jesus' miracle apparent to everyone. God can make even the smallest gift sufficient for His ministry.

CRAFTER SUPPLIES

- ☐ Paper plate
- ☐ Half a licorice stick
- ☐ Fruit leather piece, about 3" x 3"
- ☐ Bottom half of an ice-cream cone

GROUP SUPPLIES

- ☐ Bowl of fish-shaped crackers (2 per chef)
- ☐ Bowl of bread stick crackers (3 per chef)

TEACHER SUPPLIES

- ☐ Serrated knife
- ☐ Scissors

Mess Management

- Use your serrated knife to cut the bottom halves off of the ice-cream cones, one per chef.
- Cut fruit leather into pieces approximately 3" x 3" square.
- Half enough licorice sticks so that each chef can have one.
- Prepare the bowls of fish and bread stick crackers.

ALLERGY WARNING: *If you have a chef who is allergic to peanuts, handling the candy could be dangerous. Allow her to use a piece of string cheese instead of the licorice and a piece of American cheese (if no dairy allergy) instead of the fruit leather. If you have a chef who is allergic to wheat products, you can use a paper cup instead of the ice-cream cone, and gummy fish and rolled up cheese to look like a loaf of bread.*

 # Appetizer

Once, a young boy shared his whole lunch with Jesus. Then Jesus shared the boy's lunch with over 5,000 people! Can you remember a time when someone shared with you?

 # Instructions

Attach the Handle:

❶ Bend the licorice piece into an arc like a rainbow. This is the picnic basket handle. Tuck the ends into your ice-cream cone.

Add the Picnic Blanket:

❶ Carefully lay your fruit leather between the licorice handle and the cone to be the picnic blanket. Demonstrate this step.

❷ Use your finger to push the middle of the fruit leather into the cone. The blanket will drape over the two sides of the top of the cone.

Fill the Basket:

❶ Gather three bread stick crackers. Place them in your basket.

❷ Gather two fish crackers. Place them in your basket.

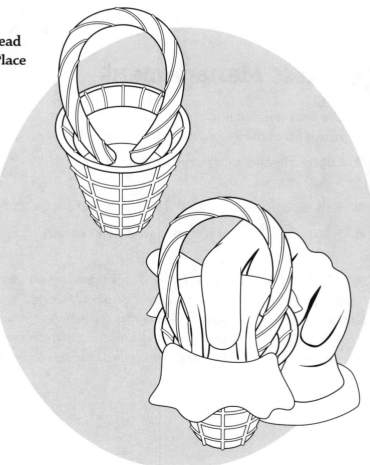

 # Dessert

- **How did Jesus help the boy share?** (Jesus made the boy's lunch into enough food to feed over 5,000 people. Jesus performed a miracle.)

- **Jesus can help us share. What can you share?** (Give children time to volunteer answers.)

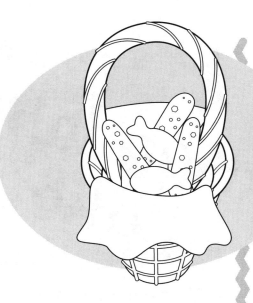

Dear Jesus, You did amazing things when You shared the boy's lunch with all those people. Sharing is sometimes hard to do. Help us to share. In Jesus' name we pray, amen.

Friendship Cake

Friends work together to fashion this friendly bug cake.

Bible Basis: John 12:1–3

MEMORY VERSE:
A friend loves at all times.
Proverbs 17:17

 ## Bible Snack

When recalling Jesus' miraculous life, it's easy to overlook His humanity. He ate. He cried. He sought out times to be alone. He had friends. His disciple John was considered Jesus' closest friend (John 13:23; 20:2). Lazarus is also someone whom Jesus especially loved (John 11:3). Lazarus' sisters, Mary and Martha, were special friends too. When Jesus visited Jerusalem, He chose to stay at their nearby home in Bethany. When Lazarus died, Jesus was moved to tears at the distress of the sisters (John 11:35–36).

About a month after Jesus raised Lazarus from the dead, Jesus was at the home of Simon the Leper (Matt. 26:6–13; Mark 14:3–9). It was the day before His triumphal entry into Jerusalem. Here we see Mary's overflowing love for Jesus. Hospitality, or the "love of strangers," as the Greek defines it, was usual conduct for Jews. Elaborate, costly preparations went into the caring for guests. Mary's gift, however, was more than this. It was a sign of self-sacrifice.

The perfume used came from the root of a plant grown in India. King Solomon extolled this beautiful fragrance in Song of Solomon 1:12 and 4:13–14. Mary didn't simply pour the perfume over Jesus' feet. She washed them. The amount of perfume she used would have cost a year's wages. This might have been her dowry. Was she thanking Jesus for bringing her brother back to life? Did she understand Jesus was soon to die? Regardless, she loved Him dearly.

CRAFTER SUPPLIES

- ☐ Paper plate

GROUP SUPPLIES

- ☐ 2 brown chocolate nonpareils (circles)
- ☐ 2 red pull-apart licorices
- ☐ Small colored candy

TEACHER SUPPLIES

- ☐ Round baking dish
- ☐ Cooking spray
- ☐ Cake mix and the required ingredients
- ☐ Icing
- ☐ Red and yellow food dye
- ☐ Knife
- ☐ Paper plates
- ☐ Forks

Mess Management

- Bake a cake. Use half the cake mix and required ingredients if you have a class of eight. Use the full cake mix for a larger class. Instead of dividing the cake mix into two cake pans, bake the mix in a rounded baking dish, at least four inches tall.

- Prepare the icing ahead of time by mixing two drops of red food coloring with two drops of yellow. Ice the cake.

- Cut one of the licorice pieces in half. Pull apart one of the halves so you have two floppy antennae. Save the other half.

- Divide the other licorice up into six pieces for the legs.

ALLERGY WARNING: *If you have a chef who is allergic to peanuts, handling the candy could be dangerous for him. A cupcake could be baked ahead of time with fruit pieces for decorations. He should be permitted to join the class while they decorate the cake, but serving him a piece would probably not be safe. If you have a chef who is allergic to wheat products, you can use crispy rice bars instead of the cake.*

 Appetizer

Jesus loved everyone, but He also had some very special friends—Mary, Martha, and Lazarus. Do you have a special friend?

 Instructions

Talk about Friendship:

Have your chefs sit in a circle on the floor or at a table with the cake in front of you.

❶ **Special friendships are made by people who do things together. What kinds of things can friends do together?** (play games, play school, bake, play dress up, etc.)

❷ **Today we are going to do something together as friends. We are going to create a cake. Each of you will get to build a part of our friendship cake.**

❸ **I am looking for quiet, attentive listeners.** Call on your chefs one by one. Hand out the cake decorations to each chef when it is his or her turn.

Create the Bug:

Allow each chef to be creative as he or she decorates. Although you will make suggestions, any candy can be used for any part of the bug. Mentally divide up the decorations so that each child will have one item to place.

Below is a suggestion of how to direct this. Insert a chef's name in front of each direction.

❶ _____ place two chocolate eyes on the cake.

❷ _____ stick each licorice antennae down into the cake over each eye.

❸ _____ lay this licorice half down the center of the bug body.

❹ _____ place three licorice legs on each side of the bug's body.

❺ _____ stick these candy spots on the bug's back.

🧁 Dessert

● **How did Mary, Martha, and Lazarus show Jesus He was a special friend?** (Martha prepared food, cleaned the house, and welcomed Jesus. Mary poured perfume on Jesus' feet and wiped them with her hair. Lazarus welcomed Jesus and ate with Him.)

● **Friends are special. How can you show your friends that they are special?** (Let children volunteer answers.)

Dear God, thank You for creating friends. Friends make life taste good! Help us to show our friends that they are special. In Jesus' name we pray, amen.

Unity Mix

Learn about unity with this tasty snack.

Bible Basis:
John 17:6-25;
Hebrews 7:24-25

MEMORY VERSE:
Jesus Christ is the same yesterday and today and forever.
Hebrews 13:8

 ## Bible Snack

The priesthood goes back to Aaron. All priests had to come from the Levitical line. They were to be without physical defect and were set apart in their dress and conduct. The priests' most important responsibility was to conduct the service on the Day of Atonement, a day when no one was permitted to work. The priest alone entered the Holy of Holies and sprinkled blood from a sacrifice onto the mercy seat, also called God's throne.

When Jesus came, He became the new and eternal High Priest (Heb. 9:11–12). He, being perfect, offered His own blood to atone for the sins of the world. He is able to continually stand before God and intercede for us (Heb. 7:25).

The prayer that Jesus spoke in this passage is the longest recorded prayer for His disciples. These are some of His most compassionate words spoken. He prays first for His 11 faithful friends. He prays that they would be filled with joy, for God's protection from evil, and for their holiness. He then prays for future believers. He asks that they would find unity. Jesus expresses that the unity of believers will draw others to the faith. These words are directly for us. Are we unified in our marriages, our families, and our churches?

CRAFTER SUPPLIES

- ☐ 1 zip-top sandwich bag
- ☐ Plastic spoon
- ☐ Paper plate

GROUP SUPPLIES

- ☐ Mini pretzels
- ☐ Mini crackers like butter crackers or graham crackers
- ☐ 3 c. popped popcorn
- ☐ Dried fruits: raisins, cranberries, apples, pineapple, apricots, etc.
- ☐ Rice cereal squares
- ☐ Candy-coated chocolates
- ☐ Disposable cups

TEACHER SUPPLIES

- ☐ Large bowls for each ingredient
- ☐ Serving spoons for each ingredients
- ☐ 1 large zip-top bag

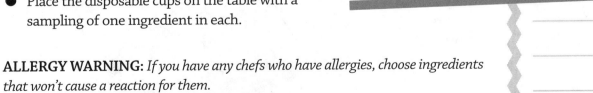

Mess Management

- Place each ingredient in a separate bowl with a large serving spoon. You should have the same number of ingredients as you do children.

- Arrange the ingredients on a table so that your chefs can take turns filling up the large bag.

- Place the disposable cups on the table with a sampling of one ingredient in each.

ALLERGY WARNING: *If you have any chefs who have allergies, choose ingredients that won't cause a reaction for them.*

 # Appetizer

Before you were even born, Jesus prayed for you. He prayed for you because He loves you. What do you think He might have prayed for? (I would know Him and love Him.)

 # Instructions

Taste Test:

❶ On the table are several cups. Take one cup and scoop a tiny spoonful from it onto your plate.

❷ Pass the cup to the person on your right.

❸ When you are given a new cup, put a tiny spoonful on your plate.

❹ When you have a spoonful of each ingredient, set the cups down.

❺ Look at the ingredients. Use your eyes, nose, a finger, and your tongue to see how they are different. Give the children one minute to explore.

Layer the Bag:

❶ Raise your hand and tell me how some of the things on your plate are different.

❷ People in families and in churches are different too. They like different things and they dislike different things.

But when you put differences together, you can get something wonderful. Jesus prayed that Christian people would be unified, that they would come together as friends.

❸ I will hold this zip-top bag. You are going to line up here. Point to where the assembly line will begin.

❹ You will each add one spoonful of an ingredient from a bowl and carefully pour it into this big bag. You should take only one spoonful from each bowl.

Shake and Share:

❶ Now I will close this bag and we will each take a turn shaking it up. While we each take a turn, we will say this rhyme:

God made us special, each and every one,
And we should work together for the glory of His Son.

❷ Now our bag is filled with different ingredients, but when they are all together, or unified, we will have a wonderful treat.

❸ Each one of you open your bag and I will come around and share some of our unity mix with you!

Dessert

● **What did Jesus pray for all people who love Him?** (Jesus prayed that they would be safe, have joy, learn about Him, and love each other.)

● **Why does Jesus pray for us?** (Jesus prays for us because He loves us.)

Dear Jesus, thank You for praying for us because You love us. Help us to get along with other Christians who are different from us. In Jesus' name we pray, amen.

Church Built of Love

Build a church of love with graham crackers and candy hearts.

Bible Basis:
Acts 20:16–38

MEMORY VERSE:
Christ is the head
of the Church.
Ephesians 5:23

 ## Bible Snack

Paul was instrumental in the establishment of church leadership. He worked passionately to spread the gospel. His hands and heart were thoroughly involved in his mission. He was humble, bold in speaking the truth, not covetous of material things, hardworking, eager to help the poor, and genuine in his care for people.

In every city where Paul preached, he appointed elders to care for the Christians' spiritual needs there (Titus 1:5). For 12 years he successfully set up several strong Christian centers throughout Asia Minor and Greece. Now he was at the end of his third missionary journey. He wanted to meet with the elders from Ephesus. However, he was trying to avoid conflict there (Acts 19:23–41).

So Paul requested the elders meet him in Miletus, 30 miles south of Ephesus. This would also allow him a more direct route to Jerusalem. He was trying to arrive there for Pentecost. Paul was bringing gifts from the churches in Asia and Greece to the believers there (Rom. 15:25–26). The Jerusalem church was under attack, and Paul was probably eager to be there to encourage them. His own interests didn't motivate him; he was constantly looking out for the interests of his fellow believers.

CRAFTER SUPPLIES

- ☐ Cupcake
- ☐ Paper plate
- ☐ Plastic knife or craft stick

GROUP SUPPLIES

- ☐ Icing
- ☐ Bowl of candy hearts
- ☐ Graham crackers

TEACHER SUPPLIES

- ☐ Serrated knife
- ☐ Muffin tins
- ☐ Cake mix and required ingredients

Mess Management

- Bake one cupcake or muffin per chef. Slice off the rounded tops so that they are flat.

- If you can't find candy hearts, use icing to draw hearts on the church.

ALLERGY WARNING: *If you have a chef who is allergic to peanuts, handling the candy could be dangerous. Allow him to use dried fruit slices instead. If you have a chef who is allergic to wheat products, you can use crispy rice cereal bars. After you make them, slice each one in half horizontally so they are thin for making the building.*

 # Appetizer

Church leaders care for God's people. They help take care of some of the needs of the people in the church. **What are some needs that people in the church might have?** (food, clothes, friends, help, learning what the Bible says, encouragement, teaching Sunday school, leading worship, etc.) **Let's build a church and talk about our church leaders.**

 # Instructions

Build the Roof:

❶ Use your plastic knife or craft stick to spread icing on the top of your cupcake.

❷ Break your graham cracker in half. Lay one half flat on top of the cupcake.

❸ Break the other graham cracker piece in half again. You should have two small rectangles.

❹ Use your plastic knife or craft stick to put icing on the long edges of each graham cracker rectangle.
Demonstrate.

❺ Lay the rectangles together so they form a triangle roof on top of the cupcake.

Decorate Your Church:

❶ Put icing on your candy hearts. Stick them to your church's roof.

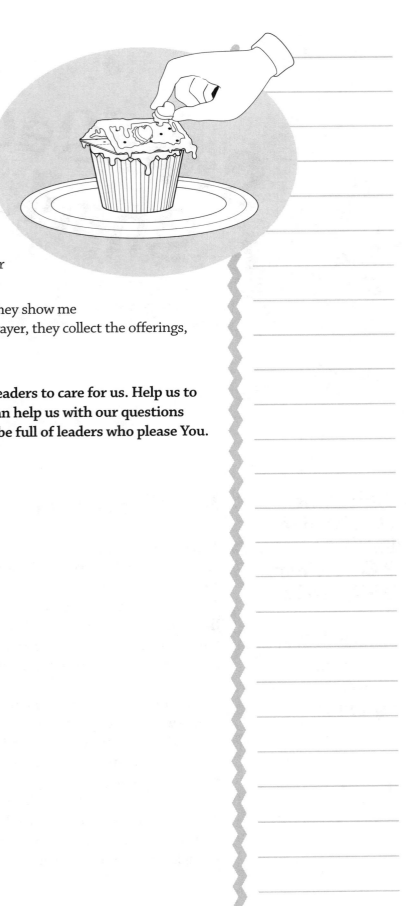

 **Dessert**

● **How did the church leaders care for people?** (They prayed and asked God to help them be church leaders that cared for God's people.)

● **How do our church leaders help you?** (they show me where my class is, they lead worship or prayer, they collect the offerings, they teach, etc.)

Dear God, thank You for giving us church leaders to care for us. Help us to remember that the leaders in our church can help us with our questions about You. We pray that our church would be full of leaders who please You. In Jesus' name we pray, amen.

Silly Sack Snack

Share this snack in your own designer sack!

Bible Basis:
1 Corinthians 16:1–3;
2 Corinthians 8:1–7; 9:7–12

MEMORY VERSE:
Love your neighbor as yourself.
Mark 12:31

 ## Bible Snack

Tithing dates all the way back to Genesis, before any laws about giving were prescribed. Abraham gave God's priest, Melchizedek, 10 percent of all the goods he obtained from battle (Gen. 14:17–20). Jacob promised a tenth to the Lord (Gen. 28:22). Then God gave the Mosaic Law. He mandated that tithing meet the needs of neighbors: the orphan, widow, foreigner, or the Levite. Giving in the early church was not based on ritual. Paul explained that individuals should decide how much they would give. However, God loves a cheerful, generous heart.

Paul took a collection for the church in Jerusalem. During that time the church was suffering from a severe famine (Acts 11:27–30). Jews who had accepted Jesus as the long awaited Messiah were ostracized. Some lost their work or their customers. So the leaders there requested that Paul help them. He spent a year taking up offerings for them as he traveled through Asia Minor and Greece (Gal. 2:9–10). Only a few churches are mentioned here. But it is likely Paul collected money from all the churches he visited. The Christians eagerly gave and even the most poor were exceedingly generous. They set a wonderful example for the future church.

CRAFTER SUPPLIES

- [ ] Paper lunch sack
- [ ] 5 oz. paper cup filled with: a cotton swab, 12" piece of yarn, 3 pieces of elbow macaroni, and 3 lentils
- [ ] 2 mini bagels
- [ ] Plastic knife or craft stick
- [ ] Scissors

GROUP SUPPLIES

- [ ] Glue in bowls (a ¼ c. should be plenty for 5 or 6 chefs)
- [ ] Tub of softened cream cheese
- [ ] Bowls of toppings for bagels: shredded carrot, dried cranberries, raisins, chocolate and/or butterscotch chips

TEACHER SUPPLIES

- [ ] Plastic wrap
- [ ] Wet wipes
- [ ] Serrated knife
- [ ] Spoons

Mess Management

- This project is intended as a gift to someone in need of food or encouragement. You might want to gather a list of shut-ins who are members of your church or residents at a nearby retirement home who don't have local relatives or family.

- Place a spoon in each bowl of toppings.

- If the mini bagels are not cut, do so before class.

- Prepare one 5 oz. paper cup per chef as specified in CRAFTER SUPPLIES.

- Once children complete the sack, remove the craft supplies from the table while they make their snack to eat.

ALLERGY WARNING: *If you have a chef who is allergic to wheat products, you can use rice cakes instead of the bagels. If you have any chefs with other allergies, choose safe ingredients for them.*

 **Appetizer**

The people in Jerusalem needed food. Other churches cheerfully gave food to them. Have you ever shared with anyone in need? What did you do?

 **Instructions**

The Snack to Share:

❶ We are going to start by making a snack to share. When we are done, we will make a snack for ourselves.

❷ Pick up one mini bagel and use your plastic knife or craft stick to spread cream cheese on one half.

❸ Pick one or two toppings and sprinkle them on your bagel halves. After you have added your topping, put the bagel back together. Let me know when you are done, and I will wrap up this snack to share. After they complete the bagels, wrap each in plastic wrap.

❹ Pick up your sack. We're going to put our bagels inside. You will get a chance to give your bag as a gift to someone in need.

The Haircut:

❶ Let's decorate our bags. Tie the yarn around the middle of your sack. Some chefs will need help with tying.

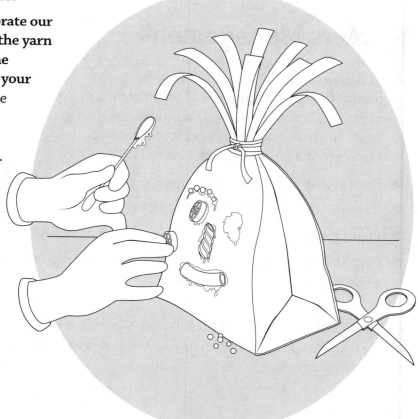

❷ Take your scissors. Begin at the top of the sack and cut down to the yarn. Make several more cuts down your bag. Demonstrate this step. **This is the super silly hair.**

The Happy Face:

❶ Dip a cotton swab in the glue. On the bottom half of the bag, make glue dots for two eyes, a nose, a mouth, and above the eyes, make two glue dots for eyebrows.

❷ Add the lentils and pasta on top of the glue.

❸ Leave your bag to dry.

The Snack to Eat:

❶ After washing your hands again, pick up your second mini bagel and spread cream cheese on it.

❷ Pick a couple of toppings and sprinkle them on your bagel.

❸ Eat one half and share one half by passing it to a friend.

Dessert

● **How did people help those in Jerusalem?** (They gave money to the people in Jerusalem so they could buy food.)

● **There are lots of ways to help people in need. Can you think of some ways to help?** (bring flowers to an older person, make a card for a sick child at the hospital, pack a snack for a homeless person, donate good used clothing, collect toothbrushes and toothpaste for shelters, etc.)

Dear God, what fun it is to share with others in need! Thank You for giving us so much that we have extra to share. Please bless our snack bags and show us who to share them with. In Jesus' name we pray, amen.

Crafty Cookin'
SCRIPTURE AND TOPIC INDEX

The following index allows you to use this book with any curriculum.
Simply find the Scripture your lesson is based on or the topic you are teaching.

Scripture	Topic	Page
Genesis 1:20–25	Creation	6
Genesis 1:26–31	Creation	10
Genesis 2:7–8, 15, 18–23	Creation	10
Genesis 6:5–22	Love, safety, salvation	14
Genesis 7:11–17, 24	God's promises, safety, salvation	14
Exodus 1:6—2:10	Family	18
Exodus 18	Family, love	22
Exodus 19:1–25	Commandments, rules	26
Exodus 20:1–17	Commandments	26
1 Kings 3:1–15	Good choices	30
2 Kings 4:8–13	Habitat, sharing	34
2 Kings 22:1–11	Bible, God's Word	38
2 Kings 23:1–3	Bible, God's Word	38
Matthew 4:18–22	Following Jesus	66
Matthew 13:55–56	God's Son, growing up	62
Matthew 16:13–17	God's Son	86
Mark 2:1–12	Friends	42
Mark 12:28–34	Love	46
Mark 12:41–44	Giving, offering, tithing	50
Luke 2:1–7	Christmas, God's Son, Jesus' birth	54
Luke 2:21–38	God's Son	58
Luke 2:40–52	God's Son, growing up	62
Luke 5:1–11	Following Jesus	66
Luke 7:36–50	Forgiveness	70
Luke 11:1–4	Prayer	74
Luke 15:1–7	Love	78
Luke 23:46—24:12	Resurrection	82
John 1:35–42	God's Son	86
John 6:5–13	Sharing	90
John 12:1–3	Friends	94
John 17:6–25	Prayer, unity	98
Acts 20:16–38	Church leaders	102
1 Corinthians 15:4–5	Resurrection	82
1 Corinthians 16:1–3	Giving, tithing	106
2 Corinthians 8:1–7; 9:7–12	Giving, tithing	106
Hebrews 7:24–25	Prayer	98

Crafty Cookin'
CORRELATION CHART

Each activity correlates to a Unit and Lesson in the curriculum lines shown below.

For further help on how to use the chart see page 5.

Craft Title	Page	Scripture Reference	David C Cook BIL LifeLINKS to God College Press Reformation Press Wesley Anglican	Echoes The Cross
Basket Boat	18	Exodus 1:6—2:10	Unit 1, Lesson 1	Unit 1, Lesson 1
Family Circles	22	Exodus 18	Unit 1, Lesson 3	Unit 1, Lesson 3
Friendship Cake	94	John 12:1–3	Unit 2, Lesson 5	Unit 2, Lesson 9
Helping Hand Prints	42	Mark 2:1–12	Unit 2, Lesson 7	Unit 2, Lesson 8
Bountiful Basket	90	John 6:5–13	Unit 2, Lesson 9	Unit 2, Lesson 5
Pleas'n Chees'n Offering	50	Mark 12:41–44	Unit 3, Lesson 11	Unit 3, Lesson 11
Church Built of Love	102	Acts 20:16–38	Unit 3, Lesson 13	Unit 3, Lesson 13
Hot Dog! It's Jesus' Birthday	54	Luke 2:1–7	Unit 4, Lesson 2	Unit 4, Lesson 2
Christ Child Crown	58	Luke 2:21–38	Unit 4, Lesson 4	Unit 4, Lesson 4
Blooming Beauty	62	Luke 2:40–52; Matthew 13:55–56	Unit 5, Lesson 6	Unit 5, Lesson 6
Go Fish!	66	Luke 5:1–11; Matthew 4:18–22	Unit 5, Lesson 8	Unit 5, Lesson 8
Ba Ba Bananas	78	Luke 15:1–7	Unit 6, Lesson 10	Unit 6, Lesson 10
White as Snowballs	70	Luke 7:36–50	Unit 6, Lesson 12	Unit 6, Lesson 12
Sweet Scepter	86	John 1:35–42; Matthew 16:13–17	Unit 8, Lesson 1	Unit 8, Lesson 7
Unity Mix	98	John 17:6–25; Hebrews 7:24–25	Unit 8, Lesson 3	Unit 8, Lesson 9
Resurrection Sunrise	82	Luke 23:46—24:12; 1 Corinthians 15:4–5	Unit 8, Lesson 5	Unit 7, Lesson 5
Cookie Faces	6	Genesis 1:20–25	Unit 7, Lesson 7	Unit 7, Lesson 2
Popcorn Ball World	10	Genesis 1:26–31; 2:7–8, 15, 18–23	Unit 7, Lesson 9	Unit 7, Lesson 3
Bread Bed Roll	34	2 Kings 4:8–13	Unit 9, Lesson 10	Unit 9, Lesson 10
Crunchy Cracker Commandments	26	Exodus 19:1–25; 20:1–17	Unit 9, Lesson 13	Unit 9, Lesson 13
Bling Bling Ring	74	Luke 11:1–4	Unit 10, Lesson 2	Unit 10, Lesson 3
Rainbow Juice	14	Genesis 6:5–22; 7:11–17, 24	Unit 10, Lesson 4	Unit 11, Lesson 6
Brownie Bible	38	2 Kings 22:1–11; 23:1–3	Unit 11, Lesson 6	Unit 11, Lesson 8
Wise Apple Owl	30	1 Kings 3:1–15	Unit 11, Lesson 8	Unit 11, Lesson 5
Fruit Puzzle	46	Mark 12:28–34	Unit 12, Lesson 10	Unit 12, Lesson 10
Silly Sack Snack	106	1 Corinthians 16:1–3; 2 Corinthians 8:1–7; 9:7–12	Unit 12, Lesson 12	Unit 12, Lesson 12

Allergy alert letter to parents:

Dear Parents,

During the next year we will be doing fun *Crafty Cookin'* in some class times. Please fill out the form below so the teacher will have it on file if your child has food allergies. Thank you for your help in ensuring that all children will have fun crafting fabulous food that ties in with our Bible lessons.

In His Name,

Children's Ministry Coordinator

Information about Child

Name: _____ Age: _____

Allergies: _____

Child reacts to ingesting allergens (typically) in this way: _____

_____

_____

Being touched/ exposed to an allergen (not just ingesting) can also cause the following allergic reaction:

_____

_____

_____

Contact Information

Father's (male guardian) name: _____ Mother's (female guardian) name: _____

Parents' or guardians' home phone number: (_____) _____

Parents' or guardians' pager, cell phone, or other way of contacting: (_____) _____

Treatment if exposed: _____

Number—in order—which to contact first:

☐ Parent/guardian (numbers listed above)   ☐ Doctor's number: (_____) _____

☐ Hospital: (_____) _____   ☐ Allergist's number: (_____) _____

☐ 911

☐ Use EpiPen—Instructions (where stored, how to administer, etc.): _____

Parents can fill out this sheet with the help and input of their allergist, and append any needed information.